讲中国的故事 听锦江声音
——天府文化安逸行

Telling Stories of China and
Listening to the Voice of Jinjiang
—A Pleasant Journey of Tianfu Culture

胡彦云　胡　萍　◎编著

本书编委会

主　编　◎　胡彦云　胡　萍
副主编　◎　蒋　兰　高　瑜
顾　问　◎　马燕生
编　委　◎　陈　倩　陈亭如　邓　珊　董　婷　董祖斌
（按拼音排序）　韩　梅　侯川美　李丹萍　李云川　刘建彬
　　　　　　　刘　坤　刘舒懋　刘奕希　卢玉梅　王　蓓
　　　　　　　王　隽　王　茹　王晓杨　谢春月　杨茂昕
　　　　　　　袁圣兰　张颖秀　钟佩玥

四川大学出版社

项目策划：唐　飞　段悟吾
责任编辑：唐　飞　王心怡
责任校对：孙明丽
封面设计：墨创文化
责任印制：王　炜

图书在版编目（CIP）数据

讲中国故事　听锦江声音：天府文化安逸行 / 胡彦云，胡萍编著. — 成都：四川大学出版社，2022.5
ISBN 978-7-5690-5157-5

Ⅰ.①讲… Ⅱ.①胡… ②胡… Ⅲ.①阅读课－中小学－教学参考资料 Ⅳ.① G624.233

中国版本图书馆 CIP 数据核字（2021）第 232201 号

书　名	讲中国故事 听锦江声音——天府文化安逸行
	JIANG ZHONGGUO GUSHI TING JINJIANG SHENGYIN——TIANFU WENHUA ANYI XING
编　著	胡彦云　胡　萍
出　版	四川大学出版社
地　址	成都市一环路南一段 24 号（610065）
发　行	四川大学出版社
书　号	ISBN 978-7-5690-5157-5
印前制作	四川胜翔数码印务设计有限公司
印　刷	四川盛图彩色印刷有限公司
成品尺寸	170mm×238mm
印　张	11.75
字　数	205 千字
版　次	2022 年 5 月第 1 版
印　次	2022 年 5 月第 1 次印刷
定　价	60.00 元

版权所有　◆　侵权必究

◆ 读者邮购本书，请与本社发行科联系。
　电话：(028)85408408/(028)85401670/
　(028)86408023　邮政编码：610065
◆ 本社图书如有印装质量问题，请寄回出版社调换。
◆ 网址：http://press.scu.edu.cn

四川大学出版社
微信公众号

序

成都，拥有"天府之国""休闲之都"美誉的历史文化名城，迈进了建设践行新发展理念的公园城市示范区的新时代。这座"雪山下的公园城市"，正以历久弥新的人文魅力吸引着海内外人士的目光。穿越千年的"成都十二月市"，小巷深处的烟火气释放出城市的自信和温度，续写着城市的文化与繁荣，让市民真切地感受到"推门就是美好生活"！这种既有味又有派、既朴野又时尚的成都地方民俗文化，是天府文化的重要组成部分，也是中华传统文化宝库中的瑰宝。在构建人类命运共同体的今天，中小学校以传统文化为载体，开展形式多样的中外人文交流和国际理解教育，这有助于培养青少年的家国情怀和国际视野，增强文化自信，学习讲好中国故事的本领，更好地向世界展现真实可亲、立体全面的中国。

2020年10月底，受教育部中外人文交流中心委托，我到成都市锦江区现场指导中外人文交流特色学校的申报工作，为锦江区教育系统的干部教师做了题为"'一带一路'建设国际化人才培养与基础教育的使命"的专题讲座，并与部分校长和教师进行了互动交流。我非常欣喜地看到锦江区将中外人文交流素养作为人才培养的重要内容，经过多年的深入研究，其在理念体系、课程建设、操作层面积淀了丰厚的实践成果。校长们展现出来的宽广的国际视野和对中外人文教育交流的独到见解让我惊喜连连。今天，锦江教育工作者用长期实践与智慧的积淀，编撰形成了具有中国风、天府韵、锦江味的中外人文教育交流课程读本。

我以为，本书有以下三个显著特色。

一是主题凸显锦江特色。本书以中国传统文化和四川民俗文化为脉络，构建起"传统戏剧""工艺文创""魅力书画""成都美食"四个主题，在内容设计上凝练了本土文化，彰显了中国传统文化的锦江表达，具有深厚的文化基因与鲜明的时代意蕴。对于海内外友校师生、在成都工作的外籍人士及子女、来蓉学习和游玩的海内外友人来说，具有典范性和适切性，是"讲好中国故事"的积极践行。

二是内容有趣，操作简易。为了让阅读者乐于了解、易于体验，本书在主题内容的选择上注重趣味性和直观性，如"传统戏剧"篇里的川剧脸谱形象、皮影戏的来源，"成都美食"篇的糖画造型和糖油果子的制作等，并通过图文并茂的方式进行呈现。在结构上，主题固化了"项目引入""项目介绍""项目任务""项目展示与评价""项目感受"五个环节，学习过程清晰，容易操作。书中的文字均以中英文双语的方式呈现，体现出了编写者的周到与用心。

三是学习方式多元创新。例如，本书主要采用项目式的方式，通过创设情景、合作交流、体验探究，让学习者易于理解，乐于参与，在实践探究中了解和认识中国传统文化。同时，以制作展示、创意表达等评价方式，引导学习者实现深度参与，进一步感受和认知中国传统文化的魅力。

人文交流是"通心工程"，要让中国传统文化在基础教育阶段"行走"起来，服务于国际化人才培养，增强中国学子的文化自信，吸引国际友人了解中国文化与价值观。我认为成都市锦江区在中外人文教育交流方面进行的深入思考和积极探索，值得学习和借鉴。

希望锦江教育工作者以此读本为良好开端，不断开拓创新，在中外青少年和海内外友人之间架起不同文化相互学习和欣赏的友谊之桥。

2022年3月于北京

序

马燕生：教育部中外人文交流教育实验区专家指导委员会常务副主任、国家语言文字工作委员会咨询委员会委员、中国联合国教科文组织全国委员会咨询专家。1977年进入国家教育部从事多边人文外交和教育外事工作，专职从事联合国教科文组织工作长达25年，曾任中国驻美国休斯敦总领事馆教育参赞、中国常驻联合国教科文组织副代表、中国驻欧盟使团首任教育文化参赞、北京外国语大学副校长、中国驻法国使馆公使衔教育参赞。先后全程参与中欧高级别人文交流对话机制和中法高级别人文交流机制筹建工作。2003年，被美国休斯敦市市长授予"荣誉市民"和"亲善大使"称号。2017年，被法国政府授予"棕榈叶学术骑士勋章"。

中国故事 听 锦江声音 ——天府文化安逸行
Telling Stories of China and Listening to the Voice of Jinjiang —A Pleasant Journey of Tianfu Culture

Preface

    Chengdu, a famous historical and cultural city known as the "Land of Abundance" and "Capital of Recreation", has a new role now as a park city demonstration area with new development philosophy. This "park city under the snow-capped mountain" is attracting people at home and abroad with its enduring cultural charm. The "Twelve-Month-Fair" through millennia and the vibrant street lifestyle are manifesting Chengdu's confidence and warmth, and continuously telling the prosperity of the city. Citizens "open their doors and walk straight into the happy and beautiful life". The local folk culture of Chengdu combined of unaffected plainity and modern fashion is an important part of Tianfu culture, and it is also a treasure of Chinese traditional culture. Today, how to build a community with a shared future for mankind is what we are tirelessly exploring. Primary and secondary schools consider traditional culture as a medium to enhance cultural exchange between China and foreign countries and to develop education for international understanding. This enhancement of cultural confidence will help cultivate patriotism and develop an international perspective in the younger generation. In this way, they can articulate the stories of China and show a comprehensive China to the world.

    At the end of October 2020, entrusted by China Center for International People-to-People Exchange, I went to Jinjiang District of Chengdu to guide the declaration work of the characteristic schools of international people-to-people exchange and presented a special lecture titled "The Mission of the Belt and Road Initiative to Build International Talent Cultivation and Basic Education" to the leaders and teachers of Jinjiang District. I also had the opportunity to interact with some school principals and teachers. I am very pleased to see that Jinjiang District of Chengdu regards the cultural exchange between China and foreign countries as an important part of talent cultivation. After years of in-depth research, Jinjiang District has accumulated rich practical achievements in system concepts, curriculum construction, and operations. I am always surprised by the school principals' broad international vision and their unique views on international people-to-people exchange between China and foreign countries. Jinjiang educators, with their years of practice and wisdom, have now compiled a book about cultural and educational exchange between China and foreign countries with Jinjiang characteristics, Tianfu charm and Chinese style.

Three features of this book:

First, the book highlights the characteristics of Jinjiang District. Based on Chinese traditional culture and Sichuan folk culture, this book consists of four themes: "Traditional Drama", "Craftsmanship and Cultural Creation", "Charming Calligraphy and Paintings", and "Chengdu's Tasty Foods". The content has integrated the local culture and Chinese traditional culture to highlight profound cultural features that are unique to Jinjiang District. This book is suitable for diverse audiences: teachers and students at home and abroad, foreign people working in Chengdu and their children, and friends coming to study and travel in Chengdu. Meanwhile, this is an active practice of "telling the stories of China well".

Second, the book is interesting to read and easy to utilize. In order to arouse the readers' interest, the book has selected intriguing themes and content, such as the facial makeup masks of Sichuan Opera and the history of shadow puppetry in the "Traditional Drama" chapter. Projects are all presented with pictures and text, such as the modeling of sugar painting and the production of Tangyou Guozi in the "Chengdu's Tasty Foods" chapter. In terms of structure, each theme is composed of five parts: project lead-in, project introduction, task, project presentation and evaluation, and reflection. The learning instructions are clear and easy to follow. The text in the book is presented in both Chinese and English, reflecting the thoughtfulness and care of the authors.

  Third, the book integrates diversified and innovative learning methods. It mainly adopts a project-based approach, which helps learners to understand and participate better through creating scenarios, cooperating, and exploring. In this way, learners will gain insights into Chinese traditional culture in practice and exploration. At the same time, through production display, creative expression and other evaluation methods, learners are guided to achieve a holistic experience and further recognize the charm of Chinese traditional culture.

  Cultural exchange is a "spiritual project", which aims to make Chinese traditional culture more "vivid" in the basic education stage and serve the cultivation of international talents. It helps enhance Chinese students' cultural confidence and attract international friends to Chinese culture and values. I think the in-depth thinking and active exploration in cultural and educational exchange between China and foreign countries of Jinjiang District are worthy of learning.

  I hope that Jinjiang educators will get off to a good start with this book and continue to innovate and build a bridge of friendship between Chinese and foreign youth and people at home and abroad so that we can learn and appreciate each other from different cultures.

Ma Yansheng
March 2022 in Beijing

序
Preface

Ma Yansheng, Executive Vice Chair of the Steering Committee of the International People-to-People Exchange Education Experimental Zones of China Center for International People-to-People Exchange, Member of the Advisory Committee of the State Language Affairs Commission, Senior Advisor to the Chinese National Commission for UNESCO. Mr. Ma joined the Ministry of Education of China in 1977, carrying various responsibilities in multilateral diplomacy in international people-to-people exchange and cooperation. He was Education Counsellor with the Chinese Consulate-General in Houston, USA, Deputy Permanent Delegate of China to UNESCO, Counsellor for Education and Culture at the Chinese Mission to the European Union, Vice-President of Beijing Foreign Studies University, and Ministry Counsellor for Education at the Chinese Embassy to France. He took an active part in the whole process of establishing the China-EU High-Level Dialogue for People-to-People Exchange and the China-France High-Level Dialogue for People-to-People Exchange. In 2003, he was appointed by the Mayor of Houston "Honorary Citizen" and "Good-Will Ambassador". In 2017, he was awarded by the French government a medal of "L'ordre des Palmes académiques".

目 录
Contents

第一单元　传统戏剧　　　001
Unit 1 Traditional Drama

第一课　锦韵川剧，唱绝四座　　　003
Jinjiang Opera, an Amazing Show

第二课　空谷清音起，一曲锦江水　　　013
Qingyin Echoes in the Valley, a Beautiful Tune of Jinjiang River

第三课　灯下的精灵——成都皮影戏　　　020
Elves under the Lights—Chengdu Shadow Puppetry

第四课　金竹合为板，中有芙蓉情　　　028
Bamboo Castanets with Copper Coins, a Deep Love for Chengdu

第二单元　工艺文创　　　035
Unit 2 Craftsmanship and Cultural Creation

第一课　巧手翻飞，创意草编　　　037
Beautiful and Creative Straw Weaving with Skillful Hands

第二课　锦江河畔，瓷竹相伴　　　048
The Porcelain Bamboo with Chengdu Features

第三课　趣味扎染　　　054
Interesting Tie-dyeing

讲中国故事 听锦江声音 ——天府文化安逸行
Telling Stories of China and Listening to the Voice of Jinjiang —A Pleasant Journey of Tianfu Culture

第四课　天府剪纸趣　　　　　　　　　　　　061
The Fun of Tianfu Paper Cutting

第五课　蜀之青铜，古韵悠悠　　　　　　　　068
Ancient Charm of Shu Bronzes

第六课　汉服黏土　　　　　　　　　　　　　073
Hanfu Clay

第七课　市树银杏走世界，天府文化放光彩　　080
Tianfu Culture Shining with Ginkgo, the City Tree of Chengdu Going into the World

第三单元　魅力书画　　　　　　　　　　087
Unit 3 Charming Calligraphy and Paintings

第一课　亲近中国书法，感受艺术魅力　　　　089
Approach Chinese Calligraphy and Appreciate Its Charm

第二课　墨韵淋漓，锦色尽致　　　　　　　　098
Wonderful Ink Painting of Jinjiang District

第三课　趣游锦江，不见不"扇"——荷香墨趣　103
Be a Fan in Jinjiang—Lotus in Ink Painting

第四课　蜀味年画，情系锦江　　　　　　　　111
Chinese New Year Paintings in Sichuan, a Taste of Jinjiang

第五课　锦江晒冬阳，好柿画成双　　　　　　119
Bathe in Winter Sunshine and Draw Persimmons in Pairs

第六课　夏日绵长，好"竹"意　　　　　　　125
Through Bamboo, Enjoy Chinese Culture

目 录

Contents

第四单元 成都美食   133
Unit 4 Chengdu Tasty Foods

第一课　唤起记忆中的甜——成都糖画   135
Refresh the Memory of Sweetness—Chengdu Sugar Painting

第二课　"锦锦"有味，"蜀"你最甜——超甜的糖油果子   143
Super Sweet Snack in Jinjiang, Sichuan—Tangyou Guozi

第三课　"锦锦"乐道，深"馅"其中——鲜美的龙抄手   149
Famous Snack with Heavy and Tasty Fillings—Delicious Long Chaoshou

第四课　甜甜蜜蜜话团圆——成都名小吃"赖汤圆"   156
Tales of Happy Reunion—Chengdu Famous Snack "Lai Tangyuan"

第五课　筋道喷香"男子汉"——成都名小吃"甜水面"   161
Chewy and Fragrant Food—Chengdu Famous Snack "Tianshui Mian"

第六课　下饭圣品——"回锅肉"   167
The Best Thing to Eat with Rice—"Twice-cooked Pork"

第一单元 传统戏剧
Unit 1 Traditional Drama

第一单元　传统戏剧
Unit 1 Traditional Drama

第一课　锦韵川剧，唱绝四座
Jinjiang Opera, an Amazing Show

你们知道这是什么吗？
Do you know what are these?

这应该是面具吧！
They should be masks!

这是脸谱，是我国艺术戏曲瑰宝川剧中的重要组成部分。不同的脸谱代表不同的人物性格。川剧变脸是川剧表演的特技之一，用于揭示剧中人物的内心及思想感情的变化。

These are Sichuan Opera facial makeup masks. This type of facial makeup masks is an important part of Sichuan Opera, a treasure of Chinese opera. Different patterns of the makeup represent different personalities. Face-changing is one of the stunts used in the performance

003

中国故事 锦江声音 ——天府文化安逸行

Telling Stories of China and Listening to the Voice of Jinjiang —A Pleasant Journey of Tianfu Culture

of Sichuan Opera, which also reflects the inner thoughts and emotions of the roles in drama.

听起来太棒了！

It sounds so great!

接下来，让我们一起来领略川剧的独特魅力吧！

Next, let's appreciate the unique charm of Sichuan Opera!

项目介绍 Project Introduction

川剧是我国五大剧种之一。它可以是一种艺术教育的途径，传承了四川传统文化艺术，展现了四川人民的审美和艺术修养。川剧在当今为世人所喜爱并传遍世界。

As one of the five major types of Chinese opera, Sichuan Opera can be an approach to art education, carrying forward Sichuan traditional culture and art, and showing the aesthetic and artistic accomplishments of Sichuan people. Sichuan Opera is now popular among people around the world.

川剧既是传统，也是时尚。如今在成都，提到川剧就得认锦江剧场这块招牌。它旁边的悦来茶园更是川内公认的"戏窝子"，可以说在成都人眼里，"悦来"就等于川剧。著名的散打评书艺人李伯清当年就是在这里说评书而一炮走红的。

Sichuan Opera is both a tradition and a fashion. Nowadays in Chengdu, it is natural for people to think of Jinjiang Theater as a famous sign when it comes to Sichuan Opera, while the Yuelai Tea Garden next to it is even recognized as the "Xiwozi" (a specialized place for opera performance) within Sichuan. It can be said that "Yuelai", where Li Boqing, a well-known storytelling artist started his show and became popular, is equivalent to Sichuan Opera in the eyes of people here.

◆ 川剧的艺术特点
The artistic features of Sichuan Opera

一、川剧行当 Sichuan Opera Roles

川剧行当指不同的角色。其中，"生"指男子，"旦"指女子，"净"指花脸，"丑"指滑稽人物。

There are different roles in Sichuan Opera, in which "Sheng" is the main male role, while female role is stated as "Dan". "Jing" is a male role with a painted face and "Chou" is a male clown role.

值得一提的是，川剧中的丑角大多指的是四川方言"妑耳朵"，其意为怕老婆、尊重女性的男人。《皮金滚灯》就凸显了"浑身都是绝技，满脸都是滑稽"的川剧丑角形象。

It is worth mentioning that "Chou" mostly refers to the "soft ears" in Sichuan dialect, which means husbands afraid of and obedient to their wives. In the drama *Rolling Lamp*, the "Chou" character highlights the image with funny expressions and extraordinary stunts.

二、川剧脸谱 Sichuan Opera Facial Makeup Masks

在表演前，演员们会在脸上勾勒图案并着色。川剧脸谱中不同的颜色或图案代表不同的人物及其性格。

Before the performance, actors of Sichuan Opera will outline the patterns and colors on their faces. Different patterns and colors represent different personalities.

蓝（绿）色：凶猛、可怖。如卢杞、恶鬼。

Blue (green): symbolizes ferocity and intractability, such as Lu Qi and evils.

黑色：正直、坦率、鲁莽。如张飞、李逵。

Black: symbolizes honesty and firmness, and sometimes temerity, such as Zhang Fei and Li Kui.

白色：奸诈、阴险。如曹操、董卓。

White: symbolizes cruel, crafty characters with authority, such as Cao Cao and Dong Zhuo.

红色：性情刚烈、忠诚耿直的人物。如关羽。

Red: symbolizes faithfulness, courage and loyalty, such as Guan Yu.

变脸是川剧神怪戏常用的手段，是表现神仙、妖怪等变化的技巧。

Face-changing is often used in Sichuan Opera to express changes of gods and monsters.

三、川剧喷火 Sichuan Opera Fire-breathing Show

"喷火"是戏曲演员的一种表演特技，一般用于描写妖魔鬼怪的角色，突出舞台效果，使其形象更加逼真，从而达到吸引观众的目的。

Fire-breathing is a kind of stunt performed by professional opera actors.

讲中国故事　听锦江声音——天府文化安逸行
Telling Stories of China and Listening to the Voice of Jinjiang —A Pleasant Journey of Tianfu Culture

It is generally used to enhance the stage effect to make the images of monsters more vivid to attract attention of the audience.

那么它的原理是怎么样的呢？表演的时候，演员嘴里含着一根管子，管子里有松香末和未完全燃尽的纸灰（纸灰烧的火候很重要，要燃尽但又不能全燃尽）。喷火的时候，演员需要点燃外部并往外吹气，这样就会有火花喷出来。

So how does it work? During the performance, the actor has a tube in his mouth with powdered rosin and virtually burn-out paper ash (the temperature of the paper ash is very important and it should be almost burn-out). When the show begins, the actor blows out air, and sparks will come out.

四、川剧身法 Sichuan Opera Body Movements

川剧身法是手、眼、腰、腿、脚、步等多方面的综合表现。

Body movements in Sichuan Opera include performance in many aspects such as hands, eyes, waist, legs, feet, steps, etc.

项目任务 Task

◇ 角色匹配
Let's match the roles

第一单元　传统戏剧
Unit 1 Traditional Drama

Sheng　Dan　Jing　Chou

Sheng　Dan　Jing　Chou

◇ 制作脸谱
Let's draw the masks

009

可提供不同的白石膏面具：有需要全新创作的白色的面具，也有只需涂色、勾线的面具，供不同基础的同学选择。

There are different white plaster masks provided to students: white masks need a new creation while the others need painting and drawing lines. Students of different levels can choose different masks.

步骤 Steps：

- 第一步：选择人物脸部的坯子。
  Step 1：Select the character's mask base.
- 第二步：在人物脸部坯子的基础上勾画我们所要的谱式。
  Step 2：Outline patterns we want on the character's mask.
- 第三步：刷漆，装配饰。
  Step 3：Paint and decorate.

◇ 选择感兴趣的身法并模仿
Let's imitate the body movements

擦眼泪
Wiping away tears

露脸
Showing up

第一单元　传统戏剧
Unit 1 Traditional Drama

犹豫
Hesitating

谋杀
Killing

选择图片中的身法，学习其动作、眼神、站姿和步态，由老师进行一对一的动作分解及教学指导。同学们自行模仿并练习，排练后开始进行表演展示。

Students choose one picture and learn the body movement of the figure, including his/her movement, expression in his/her eyes, standing posture and gait. The teacher will provide students with one-to-one help by breaking the movement down into different parts. Students can imitate and practise on their own, and perform after rehearsals.

项目展示与评价 Project Presentation and Evaluation

作品名称 Title of the work	
作品展示 Presentation	（照片粘贴 Stick the photo here）

011

讲 中国故事 听 锦江声音 ——天府文化安逸行

Telling Stories of China and Listening to the Voice of Jinjiang —A Pleasant Journey of Tianfu Culture

作品评价 Evaluation	内容维度 Content：☆☆☆☆☆
	形式维度 Form：☆☆☆☆☆

项目感受 Reflection

说一说：你对中国传统文化川剧有了什么新的了解和认识？

Share with us: what new ideas and insights do you have into traditional Chinese culture—Sichuan Opera?

第一单元　传统戏剧
Unit 1 Traditional Drama

第二课　空谷清音起，一曲锦江水

Qingyin Echoes in the Valley, a Beautiful Tune of Jinjiang River

同学们，欢迎大家来到美丽锦江。今天由我带大家走进四川清音。

Boys and Girls, welcome to our beautiful Jinjiang River. Today, please allow me to introduce Sichuan Qingyin.

四川清音是什么呀？

What is Sichuan Qingyin?

四川的国家非物质文化遗产项目种类繁多，四川清音就是其中一项。话不多说，你们听一听、看一看就知道了。

There are many projects of intangible cultural heritage in Sichuan, and Sichuan Qingyin is one of them. Let's listen to and watch it first.

任平《锦水吟》

The Humming of Jinjiang River by Ren Ping

讲中国故事 听锦江声音 ——天府文化安逸行

Telling Stories of China and Listening to the Voice of Jinjiang —A Pleasant Journey of Tianfu Culture

可是好难呀！我也可以学吗？

But it's so difficult! Can I learn it?

当然可以，请跟我来！

Of course. Please come with me!

《小放风筝》歌谱

Songbook of *Little Kite Flying*

《小放风筝》视频

Video of *Little Kite Flying*

项目介绍 Project Introduction

听了以后，你有什么感受呢？你对哪些内容感兴趣呢？让我们一起去探究吧！

How do you feel after listening? Which part are you interested in? Let's explore it together!

四川清音由小曲及四川民歌发展而成，用四川方言进行演唱，有超过100多支曲牌，迄今已有300多年的历史。2008年，四川清音作为首批入选四川省非物质文化遗产名录的项目之一，入选"国家级第二批非物质文化遗产名录"。

Developed from ballad and the folk songs, Sichuan Qingyin is sung in Sichuan dialect. It has more than 100 pieces of tunes with a history of over

300 years. In 2008, as the first batch of projects to be included in the intangible cultural heritage list of Sichuan province, Sichuan Qingyin was selected in the second batch on the national intangible cultural heritage list.

四川清音简介
An introduction to Sichuan Qingyin

四川清音被誉为"东方歌剧",演唱时最有特点的是它独有的哈哈腔和弹舌音,唱者手持鼓板,边唱边表演,声音清脆甜美。

Sichuan Qingyin is known as the "Oriental Opera". Its unique characteristics include haha tune and lingual sound. The singer sings and beats the drum board while performing in a clear and sweet voice.

◇ 代表人物
Representative

李月秋,1925年生,四川成都人。7岁拜师学唱四川清音,12岁出师后便在书场茶馆演唱,受到听众的赞誉。她擅唱的曲目有《秋江》《尼姑下山》。1957年,她参加了在莫斯科举行的第六届世界青年合唱联欢节,演唱了《小放风筝》《忆娥郎》并获得金质奖章。她将前辈创造的"呵呵腔"发展为独具特色的"哈哈腔",形成了独具特色的演唱风格。

Li Yueqiu, who was born in 1925 in Chengdu, Sichuan, learned to sing Sichuan

Qingyin from her teacher at 7 years old and began to sing in tea houses after finishing her apprenticeship at 12 years old, then she was greatly praised by the audience. Her famous works include *Autumn River* and *A Nun Is Going Downhill*. In 1957, at the 6th World Youth Chorus Festival held in Moscow, she sang *Little Kite Flying* and *Memory of My Lover*, winning the gold medal. She developed the "haha tune" from her predecessors' "hehe tune", and thereafter form a unique singing style.

✧ 四川清音的舞台表演技巧之一 —— 走圆场
One of the stage performance skills of Sichuan Qingyin — Walking around

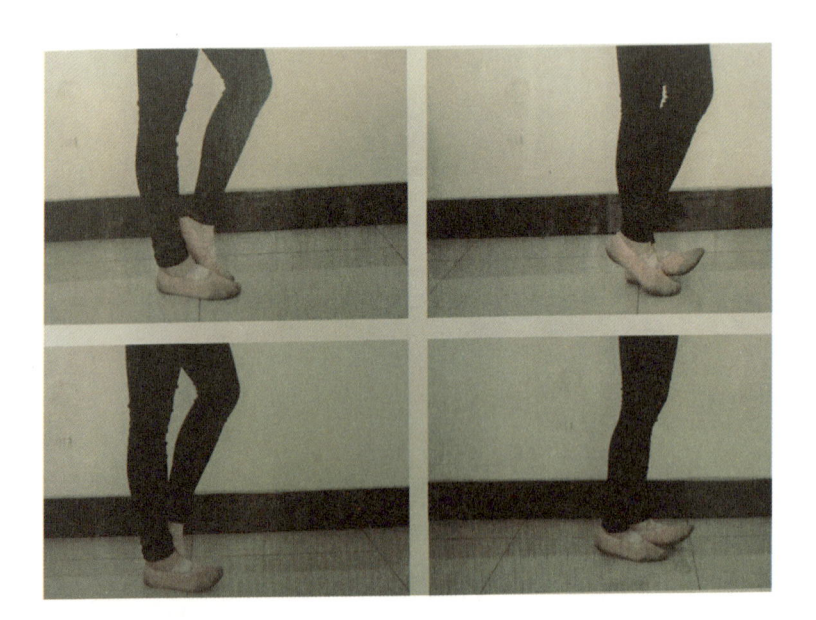

第一单元 传统戏剧
Unit 1 Traditional Drama

✧ 四川清音的手持伴奏乐器
Sichuan Qingyin's hand-held musical instruments

竹鼓
Bamboo drum

檀板
Sandalwood clapper

演员表演时左手打檀板，右手用竹签敲击竹鼓以控制节奏及演唱速度。伴奏乐器有檀板、竹节鼓、琵琶、中阮、二胡、高胡等。

During the performance, the actor plays the sandalwood clappers with his left hand and taps the bamboo drum with a bamboo stick to keep the rhythm and singing speed with her right hand. Accompaniment instruments include sandalwood clappers, bamboo drum, Pipa, Zhongruan, Erhu, Gaohu, etc.

讲 中国故事　听 锦江声音 ——天府文化安逸行
Telling Stories of China and Listening to the Voice of Jinjiang —A Pleasant Journey of Tianfu Culture

项目任务 Task

◇ **模仿乐器的演奏动作**
Imitate the actions of playing the instruments

参与体验四川清音《小放风筝》的表演，体会四川清音的风格特点。

Let's participate in the performance of Sichuan Qingyin *Little Kite Flying* to learn about the styles and characteristics of Sichuan Qingyin.

四川清音经典曲目《小放风筝》
The classic piece of Sichuan Qingyin *Little Kite Flying*

第一单元　传统戏剧
Unit 1 Traditional Drama

项目展示与评价 Project Presentation and Evaluation

作品名称 Title of the work	
作品展示 Presentation	（照片粘贴 Stick the photo here）
作品评价 Evaluation	内容维度 Content：☆☆☆☆☆ 形式维度 Form：☆☆☆☆☆

项目感受 Reflection

说一说：了解了四川清音，你有什么感受吗？

Share with us: how do you feel about Sichuan Qingyin after learning about it?

讲 中国故事　听 锦江声音　——天府文化安逸行
Telling Stories of China and Listening to the Voice of Jinjiang —A Pleasant Journey of Tianfu Culture

第三课　灯下的精灵 —— 成都皮影戏

Elves under the Lights
—Chengdu Shadow Puppetry

猜谜语　"远看像座庙,近看灯火照。里头人马喊,外头哈哈笑。"
Riddle "A temple from a distance; lights from a close look. Yells from inside; laughters from outside."

小伙伴,你知道吗?这个谜语的答案就是中国民间传统表演艺术"皮影戏"。你了解皮影戏吗?

The answer to the riddle is "shadow puppetry", a traditional Chinese performing art. Do you know about it?

记得我在法国看过皮影表演,屏上人偶的投影像电影似的。它们是一样的吗?

I remember watching a shadow puppetry show in France. The performance of the puppets on the screen was like a movie. Are they the same thing?

可以这么说,因为你看到的就是法国版的"中国皮影戏"。中国皮影戏历史悠久,是最早传入西方的中国传统艺术之一。今天我们就来感受一下中国皮影戏的独特魅力吧!

Yes, you can say that. It can be regarded as the French version of Chinese shadow puppetry. Chinese shadow puppetry has a long history, and it is one of the earliest Chinese traditional arts introduced into the Western world. Let's come and feel the unique charm of Chinese shadow puppetry.

第一单元　传统戏剧
Unit 1 Traditional Drama

项目介绍 Project Introduction

皮影戏在我国古代深受百姓喜爱。艺人在幕布背后操控戏曲人物，用当地特有的曲调唱述故事，再配以器乐，具有浓厚的乡土气息。

Shadow puppetry was popular in ancient China especially among the common people. The performers manipulated the puppets and sang the story with local tunes behind the screen. The show was also performed with instrumental music, which has a strong local feature.

1767年，皮影戏经由法国传教士带回法国，当地人称之为"中国灯影"，在巴黎、马赛的演出曾轰动一时。后经法国人改造，成为"法兰西灯影"。中国皮影戏对丰富世界艺坛作出了独特的贡献。2011年，中国皮影戏被列入人类非物质文化遗产名录。

In 1767, French missionaries brought the skills of shadow puppetry back to France, and this type of performance was called "Chinese shadow puppetry" by the local people. The shows in Paris and Marseilles have gained great popularity. After that, French craftsmen remoulded it to be the "French shadow puppetry". Chinese shadow puppetry has made a unique contribution to the art world. In 2011, Chinese shadow puppetry was included in the Representative List of the Intangible Cultural Heritage of Humanity.

原来欧洲的灯影是从中国传入的。那中国的皮影戏是怎么来的呢？
Shadow puppetry in Europe is originally from China. Then where did Chinese shadow puppetry come from?

Telling Stories of China and Listening to the Voice of Jinjiang —A Pleasant Journey of Tianfu Culture

> 皮影戏的由来，还是一个美丽的爱情故事呢。
> Chinese shadow puppetry comes from a beautiful and touching love story.

传说汉武帝爱妃李夫人病故后，武帝思念心切，神情恍惚。大臣李少翁见此，用棉帛裁成李夫人影像，晚上请见皇帝，点上烛灯，设置帷帐，在帐中表演。人影游动，仿佛李夫人再生。武帝看罢，龙颜大悦，爱不释手。皮影戏就这样诞生了。

Legend has it that Emperor Wu of Han's beloved concubine, Lady Lee, died of illness and the emperor immersed himself in grief. Seeing this, Minister Li Shaoweng made an image of Lee with cotton cloth. He went to meet the emperor at night, lighting a candle lamp and setting up a tent. Li Shaoweng performed with the puppet of Lee under the light. The animated image of Lee delighted the emperor. In this way was the shadow puppetry invented.

> 清朝年间，川西民间艺人创作出了成都皮影。
> In the Qing Dynasty, artists from western Sichuan created Chengdu shadow puppetry.

◆ 形象

Character

成都皮影吸取了陕西皮影精雕细刻的优点，而图案装饰汲取了川剧表演艺术的精华，丰富传神。其服饰华美、做工精致，配色基本以红、黄、绿、黑、白为主；影人基本都是大额头、蒜头鼻，并有上唇微翘、下颚紧收等特

征，充满智慧，又不失含蓄典雅。

Chengdu shadow puppetry has absorbed the advantages of fine carving of Shaanxi shadow puppetry, while the pattern decorations have been developed from the essence of Sichuan Opera, so that rich and vivid characters are shaped. The characters wear resplendent clothes with exquisite workmanship, and red, yellow, green, black and white are the main colors. The puppets usually have a big forehead and a fat nose with upper lip slightly warped and lower jaw retruded. The images of Chengdu shadow puppets look smart as well as elaborate.

◇ 结构
Structure

按照影人尺寸大小，成都皮影可分为"大皮影"和"中皮影"两种。大皮影身高六七十厘米，中皮影身高二三十厘米。成都皮影比北方皮影的影人高出近一倍，且活动部位更多，因此更加细腻、生动，被赞誉为"最复杂的皮影"。

According to the size, Chengdu shadow puppets can be classified into "large puppets", which are 60 to 70 cm high and "medium puppets", which are 20 to 30 cm high. Chengdu shadow puppets are usually twice the height of the northern shadow puppets. Moreover, Chengdu shadow puppets have more movable joints, making them more flexible and vivid. Thus, Chengdu shadow puppets are acclaimed as "the most complicated shadow puppets".

◇ 唱腔
Singing

成都皮影戏的唱腔跟川剧具有千丝万缕的联系，分为昆、高、胡、弹、灯五种声腔，演奏乐器有锣、鼓、二胡、三弦、梆子等。

Chengdu shadow puppetry is inextricably linked to Sichuan Opera. They both have five kinds of singing tunes, namely Kun, Gao, Hu, Tan, and Deng. Musical instruments include gong, drum, erhu, sanxian, clapper, etc.

讲中国故事 听锦江声音——天府文化安逸行
Telling Stories of China and Listening to the Voice of Jinjiang —A Pleasant Journey of Tianfu Culture

原来这就是成都皮影。我了解到它的特点有：
Now I can tell the features of Chengdu shadow puppetry:
_____
_____

项目任务 Task

"一口道尽千古事，双手挥舞百万兵。三尺生绡做戏台，全凭十指逗诙谐。"成都皮影表演过程中人数较多，既有分工又有协作，唱做结合。皮影的制作过程十分复杂，操作起来也需要极高的专业技巧。要让人物"活"起来，艺人们需要制作肢体可以灵活活动的皮影部位，再将其拼订起来。

"A voice singing thousands of stories; two hands playing millions of soldiers. A three-feet cloth making the stage; fingers performing with humor." This poem has reflected the complexity of shadow puppetry. Chengdu shadow puppetry usually needs many performers, who cooperate on the work of singing and manipulating. The puppet making process is very complex. Manipulating puppets also needs professional performing skills. To make the puppets "alive", craftsmen need to make many movable and flexible body parts and pin them together.

皮影经过起稿、雕刻、敷色、烫平、连接等多道工序制作完成。今天我们做的是简化版的皮影，需要用到剪刀、笔刷、颜料、连接环和操纵杆等工具。

Professional puppet making involves many steps such as drafting, carving, coloring, ironing and jointing. To make a simplified version of puppet, we need scissors, painting brushes, pigments, connecting rings and operating levers.

◇ 素材选配
Materials

《西游记》是中国古代四大名著之一，讲述孙悟空、猪八戒、沙僧与大唐高僧玄奘去西天取经的故事，师徒四人一路降妖伏魔，历经八十一难，取得真经，终于修成正果。

Journey to the West is one of the "Four Great Classics in Chinese history", which tells the story of Sun Wukong, Zhu Bajie, Sha Wujing, and Xuanzang, the eminent monk of Tang Dynasty going to the west for Buddhist scriptures. The four of them went through 81 hardships to get the true scriptures and finally achieved the Buddhahood.

◇ 选一位西游记角色并制作其皮影
Choose a character from Journey to the west and make a shadow puppet of it

跟着下面的步骤试一试吧。
Follow the steps below.

1. 剪出皮影部件　　2. 将部件上色　　3. 将部件组装起来
   Cutting out　　　　Coloring　　　　Assembling

讲 中国故事　听 锦江声音——天府文化安逸行
Telling Stories of China and Listening to the Voice of Jinjiang —A Pleasant Journey of Tianfu Culture

4.连接皮影与操纵杆
Connecting with the operating levers

5.组装完成
Completed

项目展示与评价 Project Presentation and Evaluation

作品名称 Title of the work	
作品展示 Presentation	（照片粘贴 Stick the photo here）
作品评价 Evaluation	内容维度 Content：☆☆☆☆☆ 形式维度 Form：☆☆☆☆☆

项目感受 Reflection

1. 通过了解皮影戏和动手制作，你知道了什么？和你的同伴交流。你也可以和同伴合作表演一段西游故事。

What have you known about shadow puppetry after learning and making shadow puppets? Please discuss in groups. You can also perform a short story from *Journey to the West* with your partners.

第一单元 传统戏剧
Unit 1 Traditional Drama

2. 你还有什么想知道的？请写下来。

What else do you want to know about shadow puppetry? Please write it down.

趣味课后 Fun After Class

想要了解更多成都皮影知识，可到以下博物馆参观。

You can visit the following museums to learn more about Chengdu shadow puppetry.

成都皮影艺术馆 Chengdu Museum of Shadow Art	成都市都江堰玉堂街道花木城梅花村74号 No. 74 Meihua Village, Huamucheng, Yutang Street, Dujiangyan District, Chengdu 周二至周日9:00-17:00 Tues.—Sun. 9:00 - 17:00
成都博物馆 Chengdu Museum	成都市青羊区小河街1号（天府广场西侧） No. 1 Xiaohe Street, Qingyang District, Chengdu (West side of Tianfu Square) 周二至周日9:00-17:00 Tues.—Sun. 9:00 - 17:00
四川博物馆 Sichuan Museum	成都市青羊区浣花南路251号 No. 251 South Huanhua Road, Qingyang District, Chengdu 周二至周日9:00-17:00 Tues.—Sun. 9:00 - 17:00

讲中国故事 听锦江声音——天府文化安逸行
Telling Stories of China and Listening to the Voice of Jinjiang —A Pleasant Journey of Tianfu Culture

第四课 金竹合为板，中有芙蓉情

Bamboo Castanets with Copper Coins, a Deep Love for Chengdu

四川有一个有趣的国家非遗项目——四川金钱板，想不想去看看？

In Sichuan, there is an interesting project of national intangible heritage — Sichuan Jinqianban. Do you want to learn about it?

四川金钱板是什么呀？

What is Sichuan Jinqianban?

四川金钱板是我们四川的一个曲艺项目，是巴蜀文化的代表之一，2008年列入国家非物质文化遗产保护名录。其幽默风趣的表演一定会让你感觉很有趣，让我先带你看一看吧！

Sichuan Jinqianban is one of the folk musical arts in Sichuan, and also one of the representatives of Ba-Shu culture. It was included in the national intangible cultural heritage list in 2008. The humorous performance of Jinqianban will definitely bring enjoyment to you. Let's have a look!

第一单元　传统戏剧
Unit 1 Traditional Drama

张徐《逛成都》

A Stroll in Chengdu by Zhang Xu

节奏感好强！看起来很难，我能学一学吗？
It is so rhythmic! It seems difficult. Can I learn it?

当然可以，请跟我走！
Of course, please come with me!

《逛成都》歌谱
Songbook of *A Stroll in Chengdu*

《逛成都》视频
Video of *A Stroll in Chengdu*

项目介绍 Project Introduction

欣赏完视频后，你有什么感受？你对哪些内容感兴趣？让我们一起去探究。

How do you feel after watching the videos? Which parts are you interested in? Let's explore it together.

四川金钱板是国家级非物质文化遗产保护项目，四川曲艺中"又说又唱"的代表曲种。演员手执三块竹板作为打击乐器边打边唱，内容多为民间故事。因竹板嵌有铜钱，故称"金钱板"。

Sichuan Jinqianban is one of the national intangible cultural heritage projects and a representative of the "speaking and singing" performances in Sichuan folk musical arts. The performer takes three bamboo castanets in hand as a percussion instrument, playing the castanets while singing. The singing content is mostly folk stories. As the bamboo castanets are embedded with copper coins, it is called "Jinqianban".

四川金钱板简介

An introduction to Sichuan Jinqianban

四川金钱板以说唱故事为主，唱词叙事性很强，有人物、有情节，曲折生动、绘声绘色；在表演上，它要求演员打（打板）、唱（演唱）、演（表演）配合协调，把故事生动传神地讲述给观众。

The main performing form of Sichuan Jinqianban is speaking and singing stories with a strong narrative style including characters and vivid plots. As for performance, it requires the actors to coordinate playing (beating the castanets), singing (telling stories), and performing (acting out), so as to narrate the stories vividly to the audience.

◇ 代表人物
Representative

张徐，国家一级演员，中国曲艺最高奖"牡丹奖"第二届得主，

第一单元 传统戏剧
Unit 1 Traditional Drama

著名四川金钱板艺术大师邹忠新的关门弟子。他在四川金钱板艺术上继承传统并有所创新，特别是在唱腔设计和表演手段上取得了显著的突破，是国家级非遗传承人，是金钱板艺术现阶段最高水平的代表人物之一。

Zhang Xu, a national first-class actor in China, a winner of the second "Peony Prize", the highest prize of Chinese folk musical art, and the last disciple of Zou Zhongxin, an outstanding master of Sichuan Jinqianban. He inherits the tradition of Jinqianban and makes innovations, especially in the ways of singing and means of performance. He is an inheritor of national intangible cultural heritage in China, and one of the highest-level representatives of Jinqianban.

✧ 四川金钱板的舞台表演技巧之一 —— 打闹台
One of the stage performing skills of Sichuan Jinqianban—Danaotai (clapping the bamboo castanets)

打闹台

Danaotai

四川金钱板手持伴奏乐器
The hand-held accompaniment instrument of Sichuan Jinqianban

金钱板
Jinqianban

表演时演员右手执两块立板,左手执一块倒板相互敲击以"得、滴、打、夸"四个基准音合成的不同节奏,配合表演者的说唱。

During the performance, the performer holds two castanets in the right hand and one castanet transversely in the left hand, and beats the castanets with different rhythms synthesized by the four basic notes of "De, Di, Da and Kua" to match the performance of speaking and singing.

第一单元　传统戏剧
Unit 1 Traditional Drama

项目任务 Task

◇ **模仿乐器的演奏动作**
Imitate the actions of playing the instruments

参与体验四川金钱板《逛成都》的表演，体会四川金钱板的风格特点。

Let's participate in the performance of Sichuan Jinqianban *A Stroll in Chengdu* to learn about the characteristics of Sichuan Jinqianban.

四川金钱板《逛成都》
Sichuan Jinqianban *A Stroll in Chengdu*

讲中国故事 听锦江声音 ——天府文化安逸行
Telling Stories of China and Listening to the Voice of Jinjiang —A Pleasant Journey of Tianfu Culture

项目展示与评价 Project Presentation and Evaluation

作品名称 Title of the work	
作品展示 Presentation	（照片粘贴 Stick the photo here）
作品评价 Evaluation	内容维度 Content：☆☆☆☆☆ 形式维度 Form：☆☆☆☆☆

项目感受 Reflection

说一说：了解了四川金钱板，你有什么感受吗？

Share with us: how do you feel about Sichuan Jingianban after learning about it?

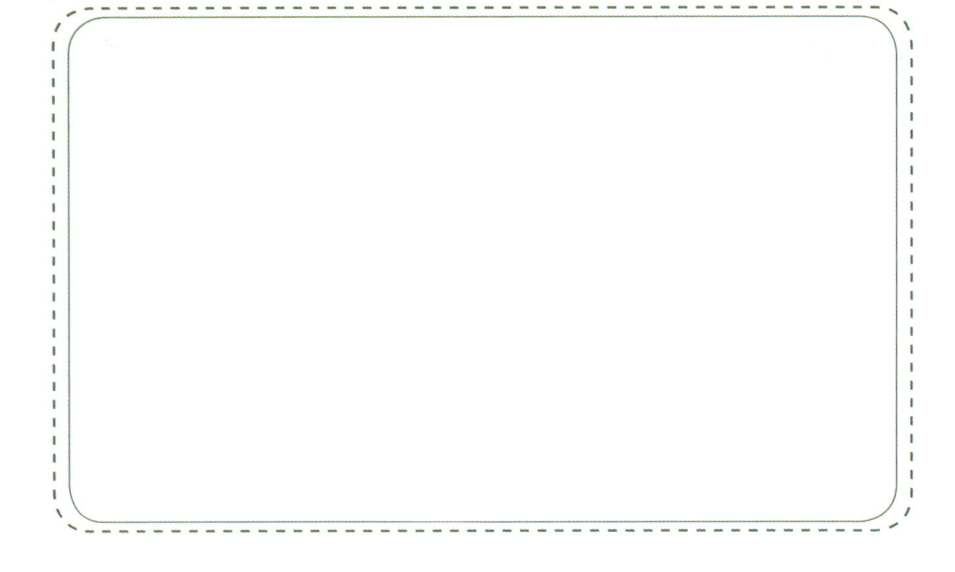

第二单元　工艺文创

Unit 2 Craftsmanship and Cultural Creation

第二单元　工艺文创
Unit 2 Craftsmanship and Cultural Creation

第一课　巧手翻飞，创意草编

Beautiful and Creative Straw Weaving with Skillful Hands

你喜欢这些美丽的作品吗？你知道它们都是什么材料组成的吗？

Do you like these beautiful works? Do you know what they are made of?

看起来就是我们生活中常见的草，对吗？

It looks like the common grass or straw in our life, right?

037

中国故事 听锦江声音 ——天府文化安逸行
Telling Stories of China and Listening to the Voice of Jinjiang —A Pleasant Journey of Tianfu Culture

> 是的，这些就是棕叶、蒲草、芦苇。这些普普通通的材料，巧手编织后，变成了一个个栩栩如生、有着生命力的艺术品。
>
> hese are bamboo leaves, rushes and reeds. Such ordinary materials have changed into lifelike art works after being skillfully woven.

项目介绍 Project Introduction

让我们先来欣赏一下草编作品吧。

Let's have a look at the straw weaving works first.

第二单元　工艺文创
Unit 2 Craftsmanship and Cultural Creation

❖ 草编的介绍
The introduction of straw weaving

草编，是古老、精巧的技艺，其出现最早可以追溯到大禹治水时脚上穿的草鞋、身上披的蓑衣。蓑草、藤条做成的草鞋防刺、防磨，棕榈制作的蓑衣防水、御寒，体现出我们祖先顺应自然、利用自然、与自然和谐共生的独特智慧。

Straw weaving is one of the oldest and most delicate art skills. It can be traced back to the time when Dayu tamed the flood. He wore the straw sandals and a coir raincoat. The sandals made of straw and rattan were resistant to thorns and abrasion, and the coir raincoat made of palm was water-proof and resisted the cold. It reflects our ancestors' unique wisdom of adapting to nature, making use of nature and living in harmony with nature.

据《礼记》记载，周代已有以莞（蒲草）编制的莞席，而且当时已有专业的"草工""作萑苇之器"。春秋战国时期，已有用萱麻和蒲草编制的斗笠。秦汉时期，草编已在民间广泛使用，且品种多样。汉代至盛唐，草编亦较发达。蒲草除了可以编制蒲衣、蒲鞋外，还有蒲草编制的蒲帆。

According to *The Book of Rites*, the Guan Matting made of Guan grass (the stems and leaves of cattail) were produced in Zhou Dynasty, and there were skillful grass/straw workers to make specific products at that time. In the Spring and Autumn and Warring States Period, there were rain hats made of linen and cattail. During Qin and Han Dynasties, many kinds of straw weaving products were widely used among people. Also, from Han Dynasty to Tang Dynasty, straw weaving developed quickly. There were clothes, shoes and even boat sails made of cattail.

草编的基本技法
The basic techniques of straw weaving

编辫法：编辫的基本方法是将若干根编材一端固定后，边上的编材分别向中间折，互相交叉挑压。

Braiding: the basic approach to braiding is to fix one end of a number of braiding materials, and fold these braiding materials to the middle respectively, picking and pressing each other crosswise.

缠绕法：缠绕的基本方法是用草茎或皮条包缠草束的芯做成缠条，缠条可以缠绕成块面或成品。

Winding: the basic approach to winding is to make the straw bundles by wrapping the core of bunches of straw with straw stalks or straps. The straw bundles can be made into block materials or finished products.

收边法：收边即是将编织好的制品沿口锁边，使其边沿牢固又美观。常见的锁边有辫子边、扭塞边、缠边、织折边、夹包边等。

Edge-closing: overlocking the edges of the finished products makes them firm and beautiful. Common types of overlocking edges are braiding, twisting, winding, folding, clipping, etc.

草编与现代生活
The straw weaving and modern life

随着时代变迁，草编的实用价值逐渐被工艺装饰价值代替。2008年，草编被列入第二批国家级非物质文化遗产名录。草编作为一种生活

第二单元　工艺文创
Unit 2 Craftsmanship and Cultural Creation

器物的制作工艺，不仅体现了民间审美情趣，还体现了传统手工艺人对和谐自然的追求以及对天然材质的充分理解和运用，使其集实用性、观赏性、艺术性于一身。

As time goes by, the practical value of straw weaving is gradually replaced by its value of decoration. In 2008, straw weaving was listed in the second batch of national intangible cultural heritage. As a craft of making living objects, straw weaving reflects not only people's aesthetic taste, but also the traditional craftsmen's pursuit of a harmonious nature and a full understanding and application of natural materials, which makes straw weaving a more practical, ornamental and artistic skill.

讲 中国故事　听 锦江声音 ——天府文化安逸行
Telling Stories of China and Listening to the Voice of Jinjiang —A Pleasant Journey of Tianfu Culture

项目任务 Task

　　来到成都，给你印象最深的是什么？想必一定是熊猫吧。让我们一起学习草编的基本技法吧，发挥我们的创意用自己的巧手编织熊猫！

　　What impressed you the most when you came to Chengdu? It must be the panda. Let's learn the basic techniques of straw weaving, and weave a panda with creativity on our own!

◇ 让我们一起来编织一顶可爱的熊猫草帽吧
  Let's make a cute panda hat together

第二单元　工艺文创
Unit 2 Craftsmanship and Cultural Creation

一、前期准备 Preparation

用清水将蒲草浸泡在大盆内或水桶里，用石头压住，使其完全浸泡在水中半小时至1小时。

Soak the leaves of cattail in the water in a large pot or a bucket, and hold them down with stones, immersing them completely in water for half an hour to 1 hour.

二、基础编织 Foundation of weaving

（1）蒲草8根，分为4组，编织十字结，每一组2根对折。第一组对折，第二组对折夹住第一组（对折的一头），第三组对折夹住第二组（对折的一头），第四组对折夹住第三组（对折的一头），穿过第一组的对折孔里并收紧。

Step 1: Divide 8 leaves of cattail into 4 groups and weave them into a cross knot with 2 leaves folded in half in each group. Fold the first group in half; fold the second group in half and clamp it at the folded end of the first group; fold the third group in half and clamp it at the folded end of the second group; fold the fourth group in half and clamp it at the folded end of the third group. Clamp it through the half-folded hole of the first group, and then tighten it.

讲 中国故事 听 锦江声音 ——天府文化安逸行
Telling Stories of China and Listening to the Voice of Jinjiang —A Pleasant Journey of Tianfu Culture

（2）左手按住，另取一根蒲草对折，挂在左上方经线上，这样就成了两根草（这是经纬编织的纬线，右手握草），经线上面的草，压住第一组经线，顺时针方向挑起第二组经线，刚才编织的这根草就在经线下面了。

Step 2: Press it with the left hand and hang another half-folded leaf on the upper left warp. This is the weft of warp and weft, and hold the grass in your right hand. Press the warp of the first group, and pick out the warp of the second group, leaving the woven leaves under the warp. Weave clockwise.

（3）拿另外一根草压第三组经线，挑起第四组经线。重复第二步并转圈。编织两圈后，把经线立起来，拿在手里编织，继续顺时针方向进行二锁编织。其间注意续草。

Step 3: Press the warp of the third group with another leaf, and then pick out the warp of the fourth group. Repeat Step 2, and turn it around. Straight up the warps after weaving two loops. Hold it in your hands, and continue the two-lock weaving clockwise. Remember to add leaves during the period.

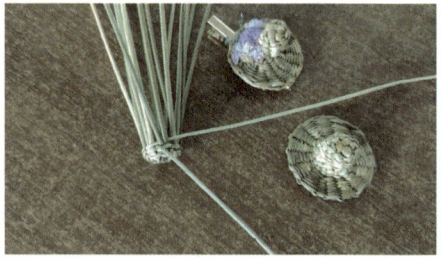

（4）把经线向外边折，放在桌面上，再分为16根经线，二锁编织两圈。

Step 4: Fold the warp outside, and then put it on the table. Divide it into 16 warps and weave two circles with two-lock weaving.

第二单元　工艺文创
Unit 2 Craftsmanship and Cultural Creation

（5）把经线留4厘米对折。经线全部对折，继续顺时针方向进行二锁编织。

Step 5: Leave 4 cm of the warp and fold it in half. Fold all the warps in half and continue to weave with two-lock weaving clockwise.

（6）顺时针方向二锁编织3厘米，把其中一根纬线穿过每一根经线的孔里，把经线拉紧。

Step 6: Weave 3 cm with two-lock weaving clockwise. Pass one of the wefts through the holes of each warp and tighten the warps.

045

（7）整理修剪，完成小草帽的编织。缝上小夹子，就是一顶装饰小草帽了。

Step 7: Trim and the small straw hat is woven. Sew a little clip on it and you've made a small decorated straw hat!

项目展示与评价 Project Presentation and Evaluation

作品名称 Title of the work	
作品展示 Presentation	（照片粘贴 Stick the photo here）
作品评价 Evaluation	内容维度 Content：☆☆☆☆☆ 形式维度 Form：☆☆☆☆☆

第二单元　工艺文创
Unit 2 Craftsmanship and Cultural Creation

项目感受 Reflection

说一说：你对草编这一传统技艺有了新的认识和了解吗？

Share with us: have you gained new insight into the traditional craft of straw weaving?

第二课　锦江河畔，瓷竹相伴

The Porcelain Bamboo with Chengdu Features

你见过编织工艺的花瓶吗？

Have you ever seen a vase with this weaving technique?

见过。这是成都地区特有的工艺品——瓷胎竹编。它将竹丝编制在白色的瓷器上，因外形精美、制作方法独特，成为我们成都特有的手工艺品。

Yes, it's Porcelain Bamboo Weaving, a unique handicraft in Chengdu. It is woven with bamboo filaments on white porcelain. Because of its exquisite appearance and unique production method, it has become a unique handicraft in Chengdu.

第二单元　工艺文创
Unit 2 Craftsmanship and Cultural Creation

项目介绍 Project Introduction

这些精美的作品是省级瓷胎竹编项目非遗传承人谭代明的作品。她在2021年被授予锦江区"濯锦工匠"称号。

These exquisite works are made by Tan Daiming, a provincial intangible cultural heritage inheritor of porcelain bamboo weaving. In 2021, she was awarded as "Jinjiang Craftswoman".

瓷胎竹编起源于清代中叶，当时主要用作贡品。现在以其纪念性、地方性成为中外宾客优选的旅游纪念品，2008年入选国家级非物质文化遗产名录。

Porcelain bamboo weaving originated in the middle of Qing Dynasty, when it was mainly used as tribute. Now, with its commemorative and local features, it has become a preferred souvenir for tourists all over the world. In 2008, it was selected into the national intangible cultural heritage list.

瓷胎竹编选用厚度仅有1~2根头发丝厚，宽度也只有4~5根发丝宽，柔软如绸的竹篾编制而成。匠人心灵手巧地创作，充分发挥五彩丝的特点，编织出千变万化、惟妙惟肖的图案。作品体现出精工细作的工匠精神，别具一格，具有视觉美感和贴近生活的实用性。

The porcelain bamboo weaving chooses bamboo filaments as soft as silk with only 1-2 hair thick and 4-5 hair wide. Through elaborate creation with multicolored filaments, the craftsmen weave them into vivid patterns. These works reflect the spirit of the craftsmen: unique style, exquisite visual design and practicality.

项目任务 Task

◇ 学习、观摩瓷胎竹编的编制过程

Learn and observe the weaving process of porcelain bamboo weaving

打底
Basing

编丝
Lacing

打锁
Locking

第二单元　工艺文创

Unit 2 Craftsmanship and Cultural Creation

◆ 编织一个属于自己的瓷胎竹编作品
Let's try porcelain bamboo weaving

Step 1：打底	Basing		
1.用排径绕瓷器一周剪出排径的长度。 Check the line diameters of the porcelain.	2.剪出的排径用镊子分成均匀的三份。 Divide the line diameters into three parts evenly with tweezers.	3.根据瓷器的高度，剪出需要数量的竹径，插入排径中。 According to the height of the porcelain, cut out the required number of bamboo diameters, and insert into the line diameters.	4.竹径全部插入排径后，用透明胶粘牢在瓷器上。 After the bamboo diameters are inserted into the line diameters, stick them firmly on the porcelain with tape.
Step 2：编丝	Lacing		
1.用一根竹丝插入竹径，这是挑一压一的编法。 Insert a bamboo filament into the bamboo diameters by way of picking one and pressing one.	2.用另一个颜色的丝编第二圈，这里挑压的竹径与第一排相反。 Use another colored filament to weave the second circle. The bamboo diameters here are opposite to the first row.	3.第三排接着第一根丝编，编法与第一圈相同。 Use the same filament to weave the third line, by the same way of the first line.	4.以此类推，编到瓷器的上部。 Repeat the previous steps, all the way to the top of the porcelain.

Telling Stories of China and Listening to the Voice of Jinjiang —A Pleasant Journey of Tianfu Culture

Step 3: 打锁	Locking		
1.取三根丝依次插入竹径。 Take three filaments and insert the bamboo diameters one by one.	2.三根竹丝依次用挑一压一的方法绕着竹径走。 Pick and press three bamboo filaments around the bamboo diameters in turn.	3.绕了两三圈后，把丝头藏进编好的丝下面，去掉多余的竹径。 After two or three turns, hide the loose filaments under the braided filaments, and remove the redundant bamboo diameters .	4.用乳白胶粘住打锁的地方。一个瓷胎竹编就完成了。 Stick the lock area with white glue. Here you go, a porcelain bamboo weaving work is done!

项目展示与评价 Project Presentation and Evaluation

作品名称 Title of the work	
作品展示 Presentation	（照片粘贴 Stick the photo here）
作品评价 Evaluation	内容维度 Content：☆☆☆☆☆ 形式维度 Form：☆☆☆☆☆

第二单元　工艺文创
Unit 2 Craftsmanship and Cultural Creation

项目感受 Reflection

我们看了视频，也了解了瓷胎竹编的历史渊源、工艺特点和编织过程，并体验了编丝。快来说说你的感受吧！

We have watched the video, learned about the origin, technical characteristics and weaving process of porcelain bamboo weaving, and experienced the weaving process. Please write down your feelings below.

第三课　趣味扎染
Interesting Tie-dyeing

你尝试过四川扎染吗？

Have you ever tried Sicuan tie-dyeing?

扎染？可以尝试，那它具体是什么呢？

Tie-dyeing? I'd like to try, but what is it?

可以这样说，扎染是一种古老的防染工艺，大家来试试吧！

Tie-dyeing is a traditional dye-resistant technique. Let's have a try!

第二单元　工艺文创
Unit 2 Craftsmanship and Cultural Creation

项目介绍　Project Introduction

请大家欣赏这些扎染作品，并思考：扎染的图案可以分为几类？它们分别有什么特点？

Please have a look at these tie-dyeing works and think about: how many kinds of patterns does tie-dyeing have? What is the feature of each kind?

（张晓平作品 by Zhang Xiaoping）

（范韵作品 by Fan Yun）

这些扎染作品线条自然，韵味天成，你了解四川扎染吗？

These works are charming with natural lines made by hand. Do you know more about Sichuan tie-dyeing?

四川扎染古称"蜀缬"，历史悠久。如今的四川扎染不但恢复了四川扎染昔日的风采，而且在继承中有所创新。其工艺特性是以针代笔、以色代墨，技艺精湛、色彩斑斓，扎痕持久、无一雷同。四川扎染技艺

055

在2008年被列入国家级非物质文化遗产代表性项目名录。

Sichuan tie-dyeing, once called "Shuxie", has a long history. Today's Sichuan tie-dyeing not only restores Sichuan tie-dyeing to its previous prosperity, but also makes innovations in techniques. Its artistic features are unique: the needles are just like pens and dyes are like ink, and the craftsmen create colorful and long-lasting works different from each other. In 2008, Sichuan tie-dyeing was added to national intangible cultural heritage list.

项目任务 Task

这么漂亮的扎染，大家想要做一做吗？

The tie-dyeing works are so beautiful. Would you like to have a try?

首先，我们来认识一下制作工具。

First, let's learn about these tools.

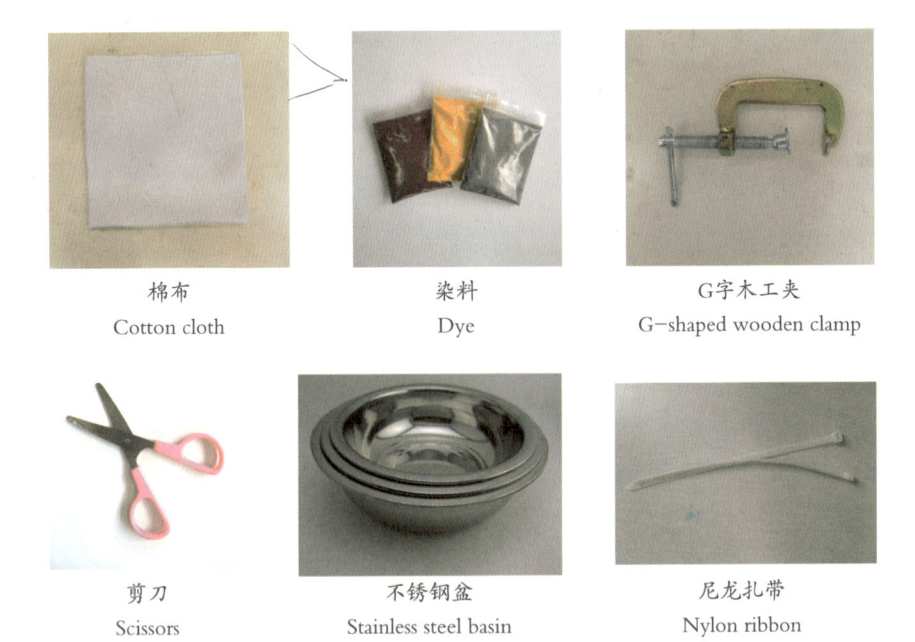

棉布	染料	G字木工夹
Cotton cloth	Dye	G-shaped wooden clamp

剪刀	不锈钢盆	尼龙扎带
Scissors	Stainless steel basin	Nylon ribbon

第二单元 工艺文创
Unit 2 Craftsmanship and Cultural Creation

木块	木板	 一次性围裙	 一次性手套
Wooden block	Board	Disposable apron	Disposable gloves

◆ 制作一件简单的扎染作品
Make a simple tie-dyeing work

（一）扎 Tieing

1. 按自己的想法折叠棉布。

Fold the cotton cloth as you like.

2. 用尼龙扎带捆住棉布的一角。

Tie one corner of the cotton cloth with the nylon ribbons.

057

3. 选择自己喜欢的木块，用G字木工夹夹住。

Choose your favorite wooden blocks and fasten them with the G-shaped wooden clamp.

4. 用尼龙扎带固定木板。

Fasten the boards with the nylon ribbons.

（二）染 Dyeing

1. 往装有沸水的不锈钢盆中加入适量染料。

Add a certain amount of dye to the boiled water in the stainless steel basin.

2. 在染液中放入捆绑好的扎染作品。

Put the tied cotton cloth into the basin.

第二单元　工艺文创
Unit 2 Craftsmanship and Cultural Creation

3．戴好一次性手套，穿好一次性围裙。用筷子捞出染好的扎染作品，并用清水冲去浮色。

Put on the disposable apron and gloves. Get the cotton cloth out of the basin with chopsticks and wash away the extra dye on it.

4．用剪刀小心拆开。

Unfold the cotton cloth with scissors carefully.

5．冲洗、晾干、熨烫。

Wash, dry and iron the cotton cloth.

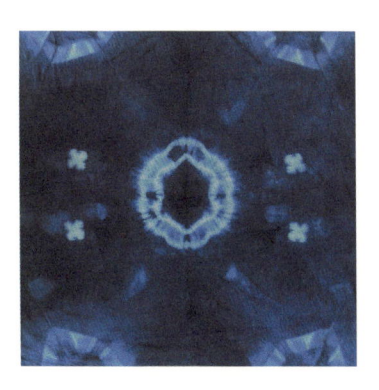

项目展示与评价 Project Presentation and Evaluation

作品名称 Title of the work	
作品展示 Presentation	（照片粘贴 Stick the photo here）
作品评价 Evaluation	内容维度 Content：☆☆☆☆☆ 形式维度 Form：☆☆☆☆☆

059

项目感受 Reflection

通过学习，根据你对扎染技艺的了解，谈谈你眼里的成都。

After learning about Sichuan tie-dyeing, please share your idea about Chengdu.

第二单元　工艺文创
Unit 2 Craftsmanship and Cultural Creation

第四课　天府剪纸趣
The Fun of Tianfu Paper Cutting

你知道"天府剪纸艺术"吗？
Do you know Tianfu paper cutting art?

我看到过，那是用剪刀和刻刀制作出来的"画"，我在很多民俗活动中见到过。
Yes, I do. I have seen the artistic works made by scissors and a carving knife in many folk activities.

对！天府剪纸艺术是一种传统民间手工艺，以纸为材料，用剪刀、刻刀来进行造型。大家来欣赏一下吧！
Exactly! Tianfu paper cutting art is a traditional folk handicraft. It uses paper as the material and scissors and a carving knife as the tools. Let's have a look!

讲中国故事 听锦江声音 ——天府文化安逸行
Telling Stories of China and Listening to the Voice of Jinjiang —A Pleasant Journey of Tianfu Culture

项目介绍 Project Introduction

◆ 剪纸的介绍
The introduction of paper cutting

《蜀戏》*Shu Drama*

《川剧佳人》*Beauty in Sichuan Opera*

《锦江小红人》*The Jinjiang Little Red Figures*

《蝴蝶》*Butterfly*

《鹿》*Deer*

《女人》*Woman*

　　这些剪纸作品造型独特优美，你们了解什么是剪纸吗？
　　天府剪纸是一种用剪刀或刻刀在纸上剪刻花纹，用于装点生活或配合其他民俗活动的民间艺术。在四川，剪纸具有广泛的群众基础，交融于各族人民的社会生活，是各种民俗活动的重要组成部分。这项艺术不仅在中国广泛流传，在外国也极具影响力。各国的剪纸艺术，由于地理环境、民俗风情以及审美需求的不同，它们的用途、样式、风格都有所差异。剪纸艺术一直被认为是中华民族传统民间艺术的瑰宝，是我国劳动人民智慧的结晶。

Tianfu paper cutting is a folk art that uses scissors or a carving knife to cut patterns out on paper to make decorations or to cooperate with other folk activities. In Sichuan, paper cutting is highly popular among ordinary people of ethnic groups, which plays an impontant part in a variety of folk activities. This art is not only widespread in China, but also extremely influential abroad. Due to different geographical environments, folk customs and aesthetic needs, the paper cutting art of different countries has different uses, patterns and styles. Paper cutting art has always been regarded as a treasure of traditional Chinese folk art and the wisdom of the Chinese working people.

✧ 剪纸的技法
Paper cutting techniques

阴刻，就是刻去表示物象结构的轮廓线，有一种强烈的对比感，图案由被剪或刻去的空白组成。

Yin carving is to carve the contour line of the object structure. It shows a strong contrast and the cut-out blanks form the patterns.

阳刻，与阴刻相反，是刻去空白部分，保留轮廓线。其图案的线条是实心的。

Yang carving, opposite to Yin carving, is to cut out the blank part and remain the contour line. The lines of the patterns are solid.

中国故事 听 锦江声音 —— 天府文化安逸行

Telling Stories of China and Listening to the Voice of Jinjiang —A Pleasant Journey of Tianfu Culture

阴刻
Yin carving

阳刻
Yang carving

◇ 剪纸技法体验
Paper cutting experience

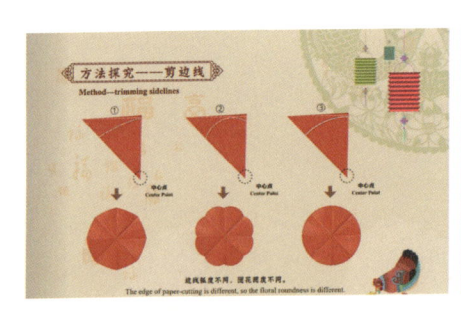

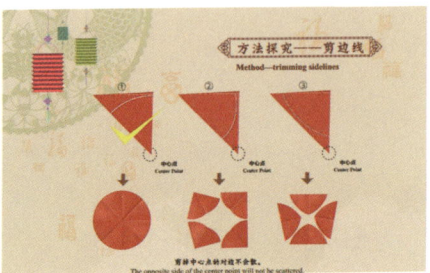

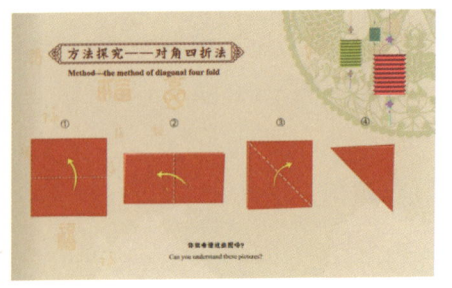

◇ 剪纸与我们的生活
Tianfu paper cutting and our life

一张纸，一把剪刀，一把刻刀，通过一些手工技法，一幅精美的

第二单元　工艺文创
Unit 2 Craftsmanship and Cultural Creation

剪纸作品就诞生了，这便是剪纸艺术的魅力。可以说，天府剪纸艺术与锦江区的联系非常密切。在成都的平常人家中、艺术场馆中、民俗活动中都能看见剪纸作品，如熊猫剪纸、梅花剪纸、团花剪纸等。剪纸为人们的文化生活增添亮丽的色彩，满足了人们的审美需求，它蕴含着形态万千的锦江元素，生动地展现了人们对生活的热爱和向往。

By using a piece of paper, a pair of scissors and a carving knife and through some manual techniques, an exquisite paper cutting work is born. This is the charm of paper cutting. It can be said that Tianfu paper cutting art is closely related to Jinjiang District. Paper cutting works, such as works of panda, plum blossom and round flower, can be seen in people's homes, art venues and folk activities in Chengdu. Paper cutting art has colored people's cultural life and met people's aesthetic needs. It contains a myriad of forms of Jinjiang elements and vividly shows people's love and yearning for a sweet life.

项目任务 Task

这么好玩的天府剪纸艺术，大家想要尝试制作吗？
Tianfu paper cutting art is so interesting. Do you want to have a try?
首先，我们来认识一下剪纸工具。
First, let's take a look at the tools.

纸	剪刀	刻刀
Paper	Scissors	Carving knife

065

◇ 制作一个简单的"团花"
Let's make a simple "round flower"

1. 你发现是怎么折的了吗？拿出你的纸试着折一折。

Have you found out how it is folded? Take out your paper and have a try.

2. 找中心点，做记号。

Find the center points and make marks.

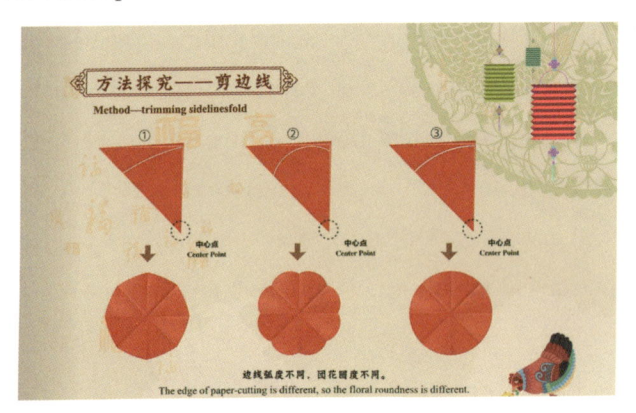

3. 方法探究——剪边线。

Method—cutting sidelines

边线弧度不同，团花圆度不同。

The shape of the sideline is different, so the roundness of the flower is different.

4. 方法探究——剪花纹。

Method—cutting patterns

第二单元　工艺文创

Unit 2 Craftsmanship and Cultural Creation

项目展示与评价 Project Presentation and Evaluation

作品名称 Title of the work	
作品展示 Presentation	（照片粘贴 Stick the photo here）
作品评价 Evaluation	内容维度 Content：☆☆☆☆☆ 形式维度 Form：☆☆☆☆☆

项目感受 Reflection

根据对天府剪纸艺术的了解，谈谈你眼里的成都。

Please talk about Chengdu through your understanding of Tianfu paper cutting.

第五课　蜀之青铜，古韵悠悠

Ancient Charm of Shu Bronzes

猜猜我是谁？
Guess who am I?

我是来自4500年前的中国青铜器，长时间深埋在土里，使我的色彩发生了变化。因氧化而变得青灰，故名青铜。

I am a bronze ware from China 4500 years ago. I was buried in the soil for a long time, as a result, my color has changed. I was called bronze for the gray color due to oxidation.

"长江文明之源"——三星堆遗址，揭示出灿烂的古蜀文明。让我们一起探究古蜀青铜器的奥秘吧！

The Sanxingdui site, the source of Yangtze River Civilization, reveals the splendid ancient Shu civilization. Let's explore the mystery of ancient Shu bronzes!

第二单元　工艺文创
Unit 2 Craftsmanship and Cultural Creation

项目介绍 Project Introduction

◇ 青铜器的用途
The Uses of bronzes

青铜器主要分为兵器、生活用具、生产工具三大类，其下又可细分为若干小类。其中食器、酒器、水器、乐器、兵器这五类是最主要和最基本的。

Bronzes are mainly divided into three categories: weapons, daily utensils and production tools. They can be further subdivided as food utensils, wine utensils, water utensils, musical instruments and weapons. These are the most important and basic.

◇ 古蜀青铜纵目面具
Ancient Shu bronze mask

古蜀青铜有着迷人的超凡想象力。青铜纵目面具造型奇特、威风，为三星堆"六大国宝"之一，其宽138厘米，高66厘米，眼睛呈柱状向外凸。一双雕有纹饰的耳朵向两侧充分展开，造型雄奇，威严四仪（数据出自三星堆博物馆官网）。

The ancient Shu bronze was created with extraordinary imagination. The bronze mask looks peculiar and powerful. It is one of the "six national treasures" of Sanxingdui, with a width of 138 cm and a height of 66 cm. The eyes are cylindrical and protruding. A pair of carved ears fully stretch to both sides, with magnificent and majestic shape (from the official website of Sanxingdui Museum).

讲 中国故事　听 锦江声音　——天府文化安逸行
Telling Stories of China and Listening to the Voice of Jinjiang —A Pleasant Journey of Tianfu Culture

◇ 青铜器与我们现代生活的联系
The relationship between bronzes and modern life

青铜人脸装饰的杯子　　　　　地铁站内墙面瓷砖装饰
Cups with bronze face　　　　Wall decoration at subway station

项目任务 Task

◇ 制作一件简单的"青铜面具"
Let's make a simple "bronze mask"

（一）准备 Preparation

1. 超轻黏土或橡皮泥 Ultra-light clay or plasticine
2. 直尺 Ruler

（二）制作 Production

1. 准备图中所示的黏土。

Prepare a yellow clay as illustrated in the picture.

第二单元　工艺文创

Unit 2 Craftsmanship and Cultural Creation

2．将最大的那块黏土压扁。

Flatten the largest piece of clay.

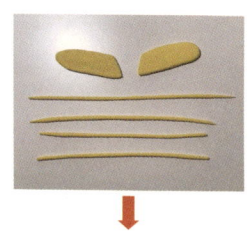

3．将黄色黏土通过压、搓的方式做成图示中的样子。

Shape the yellow clay by pressing and rubbing as illustrated in the picture.

4．用第三步骤中的黏土装饰青铜面具的五官。

Decorate the bronze mask with the clay in Step 3.

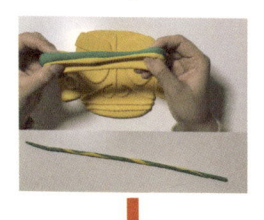

5．将黄色和绿色黏土揉搓在一起，制成彩条，过程中切勿过度揉搓。

Rub the yellow and green clay together into a colorful strip. During the process, don't rub too much.

6．将制好的彩条填充到青铜面具中，模仿铜锈斑。

Fill the finished colorful strip in the bronze mask to produce the "verdigris".

我的已经完成了，那么你的呢？
I have finished making the bronze mask, how about you?

中国故事 听 锦江声音 ——天府文化安逸行
Telling Stories of China and Listening to the Voice of Jinjiang —A Pleasant Journey of Tianfu Culture

项目展示与评价 Project Presentation and Evaluation

作品名称 Title of the work	
作品展示 Presentation	（照片粘贴 Stick the photo here）
作品评价 Evaluation	内容维度 Content：☆☆☆☆☆ 形式维度 Form：☆☆☆☆☆

项目感受 Reflection

通过本项目的学习，根据你对青铜器的了解，谈谈你眼里的古蜀青铜。

Through the study of this project, please talk about the ancient Shu bronze in your eyes based on your understanding of the bronze ware.

第二单元　工艺文创
Unit 2 Craftsmanship and Cultural Creation

第六课　汉服黏土
Hanfu Clay

你知道汉服吗？
Do you know Hanfu?

汉族人穿的衣服？还是古代人穿的衣服？
Costumes of Chinese Han people or people in ancient times?

汉服，全称是"汉民族传统服饰"，又称"汉衣冠""汉装""华服"。大家一起来学习吧！
"Hanfu" is short for "Traditional Costume of Han nationality", also called "Han Yiguan", "Hanzhuang" or "Huafu". Let's learn about it together!

讲中国故事 听锦江声音——天府文化安逸行
Telling Stories of China and Listening to the Voice of Jinjiang —A Pleasant Journey of Tianfu Culture

项目介绍 Project Introduction

请大家欣赏这些图片，说一说这些服饰与现代服装相比有什么独特之处。

Please look at the pictures below and talk about the unique characteristics of these costumes compared with the modern clothing.

这些服饰造型独特、优美，你们了解什么是汉服吗？

These costumes are special and graceful in style. Do you know about Hanfu?

汉服承载了汉族的染织绣等杰出工艺和美学，传承了30多项中国非物质文化遗产以及受保护的中国工艺美术。

Hanfu carries outstanding techniques and aesthetics of Han dyeing, weaving and embroidery. It also inherits more than 30 kinds of Chinese intangible cultural heritages and protected Chinese crafts.

✧ **汉服的文化内涵**
   The cultural connotation of Hanfu

汉服蕴涵了自然之美与深厚的文化思想。上衣下裳相连，象征天人合一、恢宏大度、公平正直、包容万物的东方美德。袖口宽大，象征天道圆融。领口直角相交代表地道方正。背后一条直缝贯通上下，象征人道正直。

Hanfu contains the beauty of nature and insightful thoughts. The upper garment connects with the lower garment, symbolizing an integration of nature and man, and also virtues like generosity, fairness and uprightness, and being all-inclusive in eastern culture. The cuffs are wide, symbolizing the harmony of nature. Necklines intersecting at right angle represents uprightness. A straight seam runs down on the back, symbolizing humanity and integrity.

✧ 汉服与我们的生活
Hanfu and our life

成都永陵博物馆是国务院1961年公布的首批全国重点文物保护单位之一，博物馆内的"二十四伎乐"文物是永陵最珍贵的文物。"二十四伎乐"是一组完整的宫廷乐队，其中舞伎2人，乐伎22人，这24人的穿着均为汉服服饰。同时，春节节目《夜游锦江》，也在锦江区合江亭上演了声光色融合一体的《伎乐·24》夜游版。

Chengdu Yongling Museum was one of the first batch of the national key cultural relics protection units in 1961. In the museum, "The Twenty-Four Gigakus" are the most precious cultural relics. It is a complete music band made up of 2 dancers and 22 musicians, and these 24 people are all dressed in Hanfu. The spring festival programme "A Night Travel along Jinjiang River", a night travel version of the drama *The Twenty-Four Gigakus*, was performed at Hejiang Pavilion in Jinjiang District at night, showing sound, light, and color in harmony.

望锦江流水悠悠，坐着画舫，听着古乐，顺江而下，欣赏沿岸美轮美奂的灯光秀，让市民和外地游客体验到美好的生活画卷。汉服作为一种民族服饰，它应是处于社会生活中的，而不应与其脱节。

The Jinjiang River running quietly, people in the painted boat enjoy the magnificent light show and classical music on the bank. The local people and visitors experience the beautiful life of Chengdu. Hanfu should be around in our life rather than being disconnected as a national costume.

"二十四伎乐"文物穿着汉服服饰
"The Twenty-Four Gigakus" dressed in Hanfu

《夜游锦江》节目在锦江区合江亭上演
"A Night Travel along Jinjiang River" performed at Hejiang Pavilion in Jinjiang District

项目任务 Task

这么好看的汉服，大家想要尝试制作吗？
Do you want to try making a beautiful costume?

第二单元　工艺文创

Unit 2 Craftsmanship and Cultural Creation

首先，我们来认识一下制作工具。

First, let's get familiar with the tools.

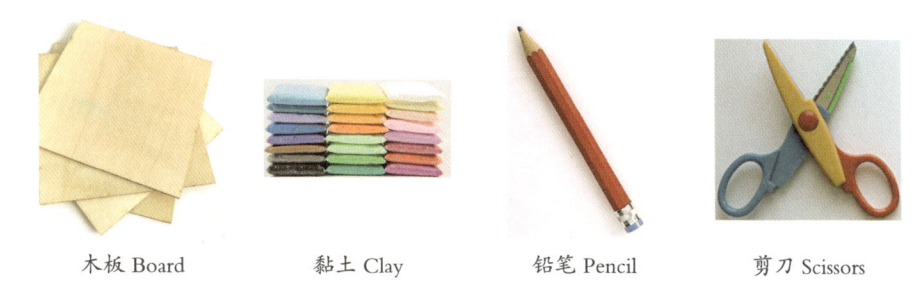

木板 Board　　　黏土 Clay　　　铅笔 Pencil　　　剪刀 Scissors

◇ 制作一个简单的汉服黏土

Let's make a simple piece of Hanfu clay

1. 先在木板上画出汉服的整体轮廓，并用剪刀剪出汉服的模板。

First, draw the outline of Hanfu on the board, and then cut the template out.

2. 在木板上用铅笔绘画出汉服的基本特征。

Second, draw the basic features of Hanfu with a pencil on the board.

3. 根据汉服模板的设计，用黏土捏出不同颜色的形状模块待用。

Third, shape the clay in different colors according to the template.

4．用小勺子的尾部或剪刀压制出不同的纹理样式。

Fourth, make different patterns by pressing with small spoons or scissors.

5．最后，将各种黏土模块贴在汉服模板上。

Finally, stick all the clays to the Hanfu template.

项目展示与评价 Project Presentation and Evaluation

作品名称 Title of the work	
作品展示 Presentation	（照片粘贴 Stick the photo here）
作品评价 Evaluation	内容维度 Content：☆☆☆☆☆ 形式维度 Form：☆☆☆☆☆

第二单元　工艺文创

Unit 2 Craftsmanship and Cultural Creation

项目感受 Reflection

通过本项目的学习，根据你对汉服的了解，谈谈你对汉服文化的感悟。

Through the study of this project, please talk about your understanding of Hanfu culture based on your knowledge of it.

第七课　市树银杏走世界，天府文化放光彩

Tianfu Culture Shining with Ginkgo, the City Tree of Chengdu Going into the World

你知道成都的市树是银杏树吗？

Do you know that the city tree of Chengdu is ginkgo?

不好意思，我不太清楚。它有什么特别之处吗？

Sorry, I don't know. Is there anything special about it?

银杏为银杏科、银杏属落叶乔木。银杏树又名"白果树""公孙树"，曾是仅遗存于我国的珍稀树种之一。

Ginkgo is a kind of deciduous tree, belonging to the ginkgo family. Ginkgo, also known as "Baiguo Tree" or "Gongsun Tree", was once one of the rarest tree species in China.

第二单元 工艺文创
Unit 2 Craftsmanship and Cultural Creation

项目介绍 Project Introduction

深秋时赏银杏对于成都人来说可是一项不可错过的活动。在锦江，有不少赏银杏的好去处。我们可以在锦江河畔与银杏不期而遇，可以在成都远洋太古里感受人来人往的热闹与银杏树下的宁静，可以在塔子山公园感受银杏的浪漫与热烈。

Enjoying the ginkgo in late autumn is an activity that people in Chengdu wouldn't miss. In Jinjiang District, there are a lot of good places for people to enjoy ginkgo trees. You can see ginkgo trees by chance on the banks of Jinjiang River. You can feel the lively atmosphere of people coming and going with the serenity of ginkgo trees in Sino-Ocean Taikoo Li Chengdu. You can also experience the romance and passion of ginkgo trees in Tazishan Park.

◇ 成都市树溯源
The origin of the city tree of Chengdu

1983年5月26日，成都市第九届人民代表大会常务委员会决定，正式确定银杏树为成都市市树，确定每年农历九月初九为成都市的"市花市树日"。

On May 26th, 1983, the Standing Committee of the Ninth Chengdu Municipal People's Congress decided to officially confirm ginkgo as the city tree of Chengdu and the ninth day of the ninth lunar month as "City Flower and City Tree Day" of Chengdu.

银杏树为何成为蓉城市树？
Why did ginkgo become the city tree of Chengdu?

（1）成都与银杏的历史渊源悠久。
Chengdu has a long history with ginkgo trees.

关于"白果"（银杏果实）之名的由来，在成都本地曾有一段传说。

There is a story in Chengdu about the origin of the name "Baiguo" (the ginkgo fruit).

"白果"之名的由来
The Story of "BaiGuo"

（2）成都古树多银杏，今赏银杏去处多。

There are many old ginkgo trees in Chengdu, and we have many places to enjoy the scenery of ginkgo trees nowadays.

据调查，成都现存的古银杏树有2000余株。其中，百花潭公园中的一株有1700年树龄的古银杏树是主城区内最古老的，虽然它经历了火焚、雷击，又从汶川县漩口镇的观音寺移植到成都市区的百花潭公园，但在园林专家的精心培育下，如今却依然枝繁叶茂。在成都最古老的树的排名中，银杏树就占了8株，当中最古老的银杏树位于都江堰青城山天师洞，有着2500年树龄。

According to an investigation, there are more than 2,000 ancient ginkgo trees nowadays in Chengdu. The 1700-year-old ginkgo tree, also the oldest in the main urban areas of Chengdu is located in Baihuatan Park. Though it has suffered from a fire and lightning, and was transplanted from the Guanyin Temple in Xuankou Town, Wenchuan County, it is still flourishing with careful cultivation by the experts today. Moreover, among the ten oldest trees in Chengdu, eight of them are ginkgo trees. The oldest ginkgo tree in Chengdu is located in Tianshi Cave, Qingcheng Mountain, Dujiangyan, with an age of 2,500 years.

白果林小区、银杏路、成都市首条银杏文化街区——锦绣街和锦绣巷等，都是如今观赏银杏的好去处。

Nowadays, there are many good places to enjoy ginkgo trees in Chengdu, such as Baiguolin Community, Ginkgo Road, and the first ginkgo culture block in Chengdu—Jinxiu Street and Jinxiu Lane.

（3）银杏树具有较高的景观价值和丰富的象征意义。

Ginkgo trees enjoy a high sight value and rich symbolic meanings.

银杏夏日绿油油，秋日里来金灿灿，是美化街道的经济林木，具有很高的观赏价值。因为它从种植到收获果实需要数十年，所以有健康长寿、吉祥幸福的寓意。

In summer the ginkgo trees are green, while in autumn they are golden. They are the trees to beautify the streets at a low cost and with a high sight value. Since it takes decades from tree planting to fruit harvesting, the ginkgo trees have the symbolic meanings of health, longevity, happiness and good luck.

正因如此，在成都的大街小巷都能看到成都人喜爱的银杏树，它逐渐成为成都的一张名片。

For this reason, the ginkgo tree, which is regarded as Chengdu people's favorite tree and can be seen in many streets and alleys in Chengdu, has gradually become a business card of Chengdu City.

讲 中国故事　听 锦江声音 ——天府文化安逸行
Telling Stories of China and Listening to the Voice of Jinjiang —A Pleasant Journey of Tianfu Culture

✧ **解构银杏 —— 银杏的根、茎、叶、实**

The structure of the ginkgo tree—roots, stems, leaves and fruits

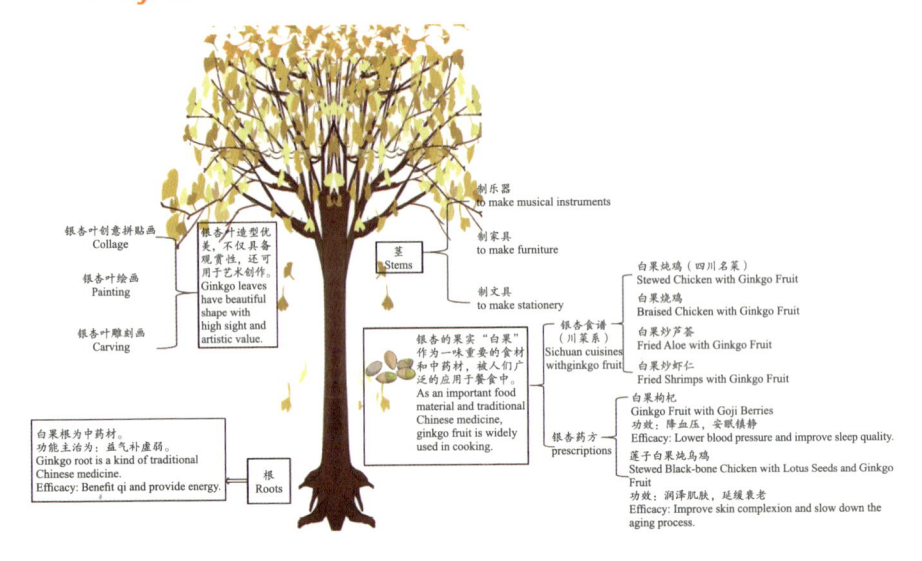

银杏叶创意拼贴画
Collage

银杏叶绘画
Painting

银杏叶雕刻画
Carving

银杏叶造型优美，不仅具备观赏性，还可用于艺术创作。
Ginkgo leaves have beautiful shape with high sight and artistic value.

白果根为中药材。
功能主治为：益气朴虚弱。
Ginkgo root is a kind of traditional Chinese medicine.
Efficacy: Benefit qi and provide energy.

根
Roots

茎
Stems

制乐器
to make musical instruments

制家具
to make furniture

制文具
to make stationery

银杏的果实"白果"作为一味重要的食材和中药材，被人们广泛的应用于餐食中。
As an important food material and traditional Chinese medicine, ginkgo fruit is widely used in cooking.

银杏食谱（川菜系）
Sichuan cuisines with ginkgo fruit

白果烧鸡（四川名菜）
Stewed Chicken with Ginkgo Fruit

白果烧鸡
Braised Chicken with Ginkgo Fruit

白果炒芦荟
Fried Aloe with Ginkgo Fruit

白果炒虾仁
Fried Shrimps with Ginkgo Fruit

银杏药方
prescriptions

白果枸杞
Ginkgo Fruit with Goji Berries
功效：降血压，安眠镇静
Efficacy: Lower blood pressure and improve sleep quality.

莲子白果乌鸡
Stewed Black-bone Chicken with Lotus Seeds and Ginkgo Fruit
功效：润泽肌肤，延缓衰老
Efficacy: Improve skin complexion and slow down the aging process.

▰ 项目任务 Task

✧ **用银杏叶来装饰下面这些锦江特色建筑与景点的图片**

Let's decorate the following pictures of landmarks and scenic spots in Jinjiang District with ginkgo leaves

内容： 由队长分别安排人员，寻找校园中的银杏叶，经过小组内讨论及设计，从下列线描背景图中选一幅进行装饰，最后对设计意图进行说明。

Content: the group leader arranges members to collect ginkgo leaves on campus. After discussing and designing, the group decorates one of the following pictures and explains your design ideas.

材料： 线描背景图（锦江特色建筑及景点）、剪刀、美工刀、彩笔、记号笔、双面胶。

Materials: line drawings of landmarks and scenic spots in Jinjiang

第二单元　工艺文创
Unit 2 Craftsmanship and Cultural Creation

District, scissors, craft knives, coloured pens, markers, and double-sided tape.

温馨提示(Tips)
使用剪刀、美工刀时要注意安全哦！
Please be careful with scissors and knives!

1. 要求　Requirements

利用工具对银杏叶进行裁剪和绘画，注意构图。

Tools can be used to cut and to paint the ginkgo leaves. Please pay attention to the composition of the picture.

2. 思考　Consideration

你可以用哪些方式来装饰你的作品呢？

In what ways can you decorate your work?

085

讲中国故事 听锦江声音 ——天府文化安逸行
Telling Stories of China and Listening to the Voice of Jinjiang —A Pleasant Journey of Tianfu Culture

项目展示与评价 Project Presentation and Evaluation

作品名称 Title of the work	
作品展示 Presentation	（照片粘贴 Stick the photo here）
作品评价 Evaluation	内容维度 Content：☆☆☆☆☆ 形式维度 Form：☆☆☆☆☆

项目感受 Reflection

通过本项目的学习，谈谈你对银杏的认识。

Through the study of this project, please talk about your understanding of the ginkgo tree.

第三单元　魅力书画
Unit 3 Charming Calligraphy and Paintings

第三单元　魅力书画
Unit 3 Charming Calligraphy and Paintings

第一课　亲近中国书法，感受艺术魅力

Approach Chinese Calligraphy and Appreciate Its Charm

一张洁白宣纸，一支锥形毛笔，一只盛墨砚台。灵动的巧手或提或按、或顿或挫、或疾或缓，运笔的巧妙混合水墨的丰富，在纸面上形成魅力无穷的黑白艺术，这就是中国书法。你感受过中国书法的艺术魅力吗？

With a hand raising or pressing, pausing or transitioning, quickening or slowing, Chinese calligraphy artfully combines ink and wash, and demonstrates amazing black-and-white art by using just a piece of clean rice paper, a tapered brush pen and an inkstone. Have you ever felt the charm of Chinese calligraphy?

何谓"中国书法艺术魅力"？

What is "the charm of Chinese calligraphy"?

中国书法在笔法、字法、章法上具有独特魅力，通过几千年的传承与创新，成为中华民族的文化瑰宝，是一门独特的造型艺术。大家来感受一下吧！

Being inherited and innovated for thousands of years, Chinese calligraphy, as a unique type of plastic art, shows its charm in

089

讲中国故事 听锦江声音 ——天府文化安逸行
Telling Stories of China and Listening to the Voice of Jinjiang —A Pleasant Journey of Tianfu Culture

> handwriting techniques, character-writing techniques and composition techniques. It has become a distinctive Chinese cultural treasure. Let's appreciate it together!

项目介绍 Project Introduction

我们以中国书法艺术代表作品之一《兰亭序》为例，来感受书法艺术的魅力。

Taking one of the Chinese calligraphy masterpieces *Lan Ting Preface* as an example, let's appreciate the charm of Chinese calligraphy.

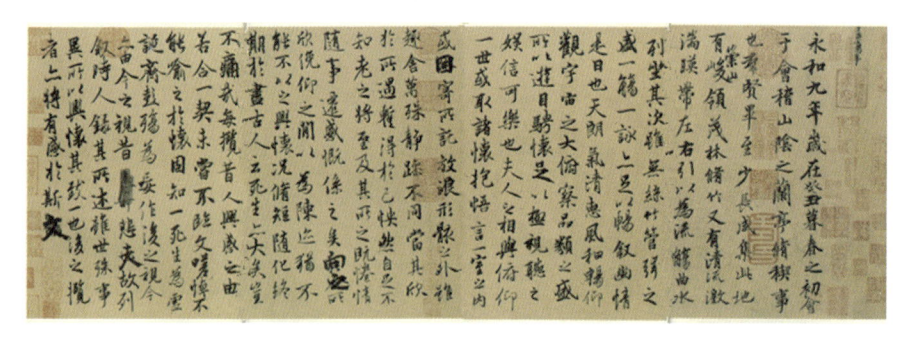

《兰亭序》共三百二十四字，是被王羲之创造出的有生命的个体形象，各有筋骨血肉，各具神韵个性，宛如曼妙的万物。

There are 324 characters in *Lan Ting Preface*, and each character is an individual living image created by calligrapher Wang Xizhi. They are lively with their own ways of construction and personalities.

序中二十多个"之"字，无一雷同，各具风韵；章法布局巧夺天工，灵动妩媚；在方寸之间展示奇妙的艺术美，充分体现了中国书法的艺术魅力。

The character "Zhi" (之) is written in different ways and in unique styles in the preface for more than 20 times. Its composition and structure are so skillful that they look natural. Every character in it fully demonstrates the charm of Chinese calligraphy.

第三单元　魅力书画
Unit 3 Charming Calligraphy and Paintings

"视"字点如高山坠石，势危力足。
The first stroke in character "Shi" (视) seems like a falling rock from a high mountain, dangerous but powerful.

"者"字横画如千里阵云，若隐若现，短横于无形为有形。
The horizontal strokes in "Zhe" (者) resemble hazy distant clouds, while shorter ones blur in shape.

"九"字撇犹如砍断犀牛之角一样强劲无比。
The stroke to the left in "Jiu" (九) is as sharp as the broken horn of rhinoceros.

"天"字捺如电闪雷鸣，海浪冲天，力大无穷。
The stroke to the right in "Tian" (天) is as powerful as lightning and thunder, and waves in the ocean.

中国故事 听锦江声音 ——天府文化安逸行
Telling Stories of China and Listening to the Voice of Jinjiang —A Pleasant Journey of Tianfu Culture

"盛"字"戈"如弩弓蓄势待发。
The component character "Ge"(戈) in character "Sheng"(盛) resembles a crossbow ready to shoot.

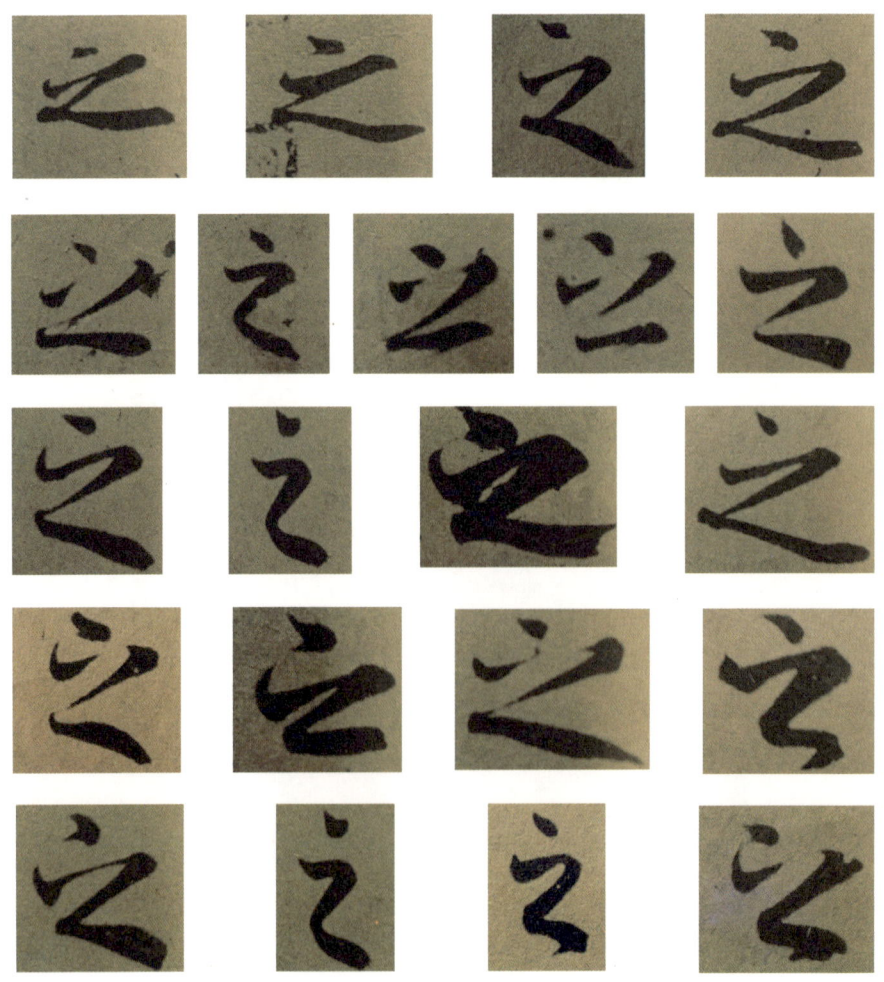

"之"字姿态各异，各具特色，无一雷同。
The character "Zhi"(之) has different shapes with different features.

第三单元　魅力书画
Unit 3 Charming Calligraphy and Paintings

结体上险绝倚正如"湍"字，势如叠石，险中求稳。
The composition of character "Tuan" (湍) is similar to its Chinese meaning which resembles the overlapping stones, dangerous but stable.

"所"字和谐呼应，穿插互动。
The two components of character "Suo" (所) are harmonious, interacting with each other.

章法上虚实结合。
The real combines the virtual in the overall layout.

项目任务 Task

◇中国书法博大精深，独具魅力，我们来书写一下吧！
Chinese calligraphy is profound and charming. Let's have a try!

首先，我们来认识一下书写工具。
First, let's take a look at the writing tools.

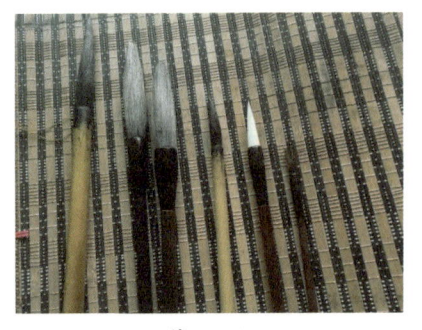

Telling Stories of China and Listening to the Voice of Jinjiang —A Pleasant Journey of Tianfu Culture

笔 Brush

墨 Ink

纸 Rice paper

砚 Inkstone

（一）准备 Preparation

1. 准备"笔、墨、纸、砚"。中国书法的工具和材料基本上是由笔、墨、纸、砚构成的，人们通常把它们称为"文房四宝"。

Prepare the "Four Treasures of Study" — brush, ink, rice paper and inkstone. They are the basic tools and materials of Chinese calligraphy.

2. 执笔训练。书法讲究执笔方法：两臂张开，左手按纸，右手执笔，指实掌虚。

Practice holding the brush. There are requirements for holding the brush: stretch your arms, use your left arm to press the rice paper and the right one to hold the brush. When holding the brush, your palm should be empty and each finger cooperates with each other to hold the brush tightly.

（二）书写 Writing

1. 你可以临摹下列楷书，做到笔画简洁；或者临摹小篆，力争使线

第三单元　魅力书画
Unit 3 Charming Calligraphy and Paintings

条平稳。

You can try to imitate the following regular scripts and make your strokes smooth, or you can imitate the following seal characters and make the strokes stable.

楷书结构平稳
Regular scripts with stable structure

小篆左右对称
Seal characters with bilateral symmetry

2. 将下列各字左右两部分之间的穿插避让处标注出来。
Label the separate parts of the following characters.

讲中国故事 听锦江声音 ——天府文化安逸行
Telling Stories of China and Listening to the Voice of Jinjiang —A Pleasant Journey of Tianfu Culture

穿插避让
Alternate and separate

项目展示与评价 Project Presentation and Evaluation

作品名称 Title of the work	
作品展示 Presentation	（照片粘贴 Stick the photo here）
作品评价 Evaluation	内容维度 Content：☆☆☆☆☆ 形式维度 Form：☆☆☆☆☆

096

第三单元　魅力书画
Unit 3 Charming Calligraphy and Paintings

项目感受 Reflection

1. 通过对中国汉字的书写，你知道了些什么？请和你的同伴交流。

What have you learned by writing Chinese characters? Please communicate with your partner.

2. 你对中国书法艺术魅力有哪些认识？请你谈谈。

What is your opinion about the charm of Chinese calligraphy?

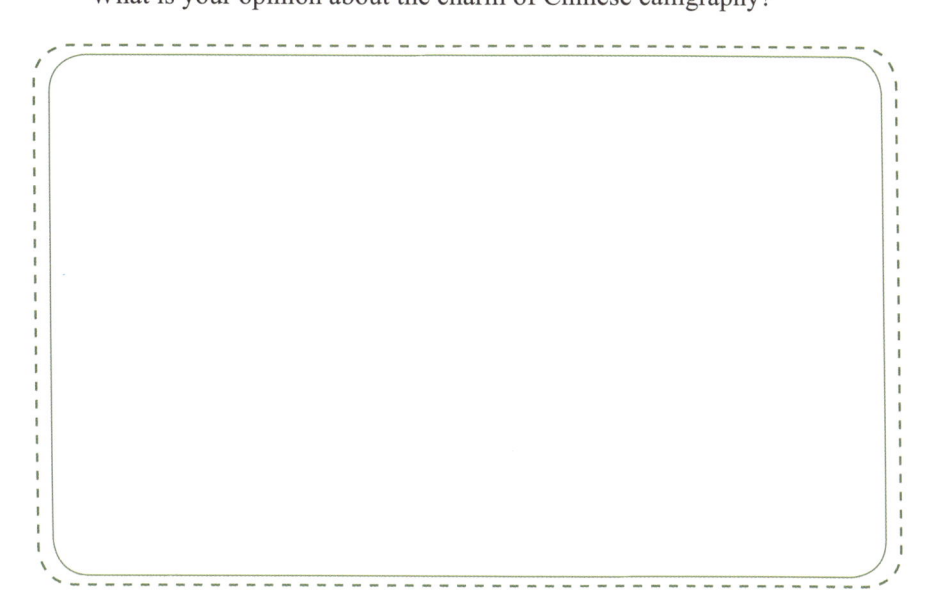

第二课　墨韵淋漓，锦色尽致
Wonderful Ink Painting of Jinjiang District

现代绘画大师毕加索看到齐白石的画作时说："中国画真神奇。齐先生画水中的鱼儿，没有一点色、一根线去画水，却使人看到了江河，嗅到了水的清香。"

When Picasso, a master of modern painting, saw Qi Baishi's works, he said, "Chinese painting is really amazing. Mr. Qi painted the fish without a bit of color or a line of water, but we can see the river and smell the fragrance."

真神奇！中国画是怎么做到这样的呢？

It's really amazing! How does Chinese painting bring elements to life?

中国画的魅力就在于以水墨为主，略施淡彩，便能达到神形兼备的效果。

The charm of Chinese painting lies in the painting techniques. It uses black ink in different concentrations and a bit of light color to get a good combination of artistic form and spirit of the painted object.

第三单元 魅力书画
Unit 3 Charming Calligraphy and Paintings

项目介绍 Project Introduction

◆ 中国画的介绍
The introduction of Chinese painting

中国绘画是中国文化的重要组成部分，根植于民族文化的土壤之中。水墨之韵在于用毛笔、墨汁、宣纸绘出不拘泥于形似的神似，具有高度的概括力和想象力。

Deeply rooted in the soil of national culture, Chinese painting is a vital part of the traditional Chinese culture. The ink painting is created by using a brush, ink and rice paper, not being constrained to appearance or form, but paying attention to expressions in spirit and imagination.

中西方绘画的对比。

Contrast between Chinese painting and western painting.

西方绘画的显著特征是写实性强。油画作品充分体现西方传统油画重明暗、色彩、造型、真实再现的特征。

Realism is the most distinctive feature of western painting. The oil paintings fully reflect the characteristics of the traditional western painting, which emphasize light and shade contrast, color, shape, and realistic representation of the painted object.

水墨之韵在于抒情。

Chinese painting focuses on conveying one's emotions.

苏东坡先生触景生情，忍不住抒发"江汉西来，高楼下、蒲萄深碧。犹自带、岷峨云浪，锦江春色"，表达对家乡的思念。锦江是一处景色迷人的宜居之地。东门码头、幸福梅林、锦江绿道、荷塘月色等景点富有诗情画意的意境，就像一幅美丽的水墨画卷。

Su Dongpo could not help but write the lines when the scenery stirred up his homesickness: "The Yangtze River rushes straight down from the west, and the vast river is as clear and turquoise as the grape when looked down from Yellow Crane Tower. The Yangtze River originates from the snowy Minshan Mountain and Mount Emei, which reveals the spring scenery of the Jinjiang River." Jinjiang, with stunning scenery, is a pleasant place to live. Picturesque and poetic scenic spots such as Dongmen Pier, Happy Plum Forest, Jinjiang Greenway and Moonlight over the Lotus Pond are dotted on this lifelike scroll of ink painting.

项目任务 Task

◇ 制作一把有锦江美景的国画扇子

Make a paper fan with ink painting of the beautiful scenery of Jinjiang

步骤一：选择下面其中一种方法完成扇面的图案绘制。

Step 1: Choose one of the following methods to draw the fan.

方法1：用滴墨拓印法画水润景色。

Method 1: Draw the scenery by dropping ink and rubbing.

 1. 准备墨汁和干净的平口盘子，滴入墨汁，用宣纸进行拓印。Prepare ink and a clean and flat plate, drop the ink into the plate, and use rice paper to rub.	 2. 用拓印法构图。Make composition of the picture by rubbing.	 3. 点景。Embellish the picture.	 4. 在扇面上创作。Draw on the fan.

第三单元 魅力书画
Unit 3 Charming Calligraphy and Paintings

方法2：用泼彩法画锦色荷花。

Method 2: Draw lotus flower by splashing colors.

 1. 尝试用两种国画色彩撞色。 Try to use two contrastive colors.	 2. 选择合适的位置构图。 Choose the right place for composition.	 3. 勾勒荷花。 Outline the lotus flower.	 4. 在扇面上创作。 Draw on the fan.

方法3：用特殊工具画幸福梅林。

Method 3: Draw Happy Plum Forest with special tools.

 1. 观察材料特点。 Observe the materials.	 2. 尝试材料肌理。 Feel the material texture of the materials.	 3. 选择合适的材料进行表现。 Choose the right material for painting.	 4. 在扇面上创作。 Draw on the fan.

步骤二：按照以下方法，把画好的扇面制作成扇子。

Step 2: Make a fan following the method below.

 折 Fold the fan sector.	 穿 Put the fan rib in.	 粘 Stick the fan sector with the fan rib.	 完成制作 The fan is made.

101

讲 中国故事 听 锦江声音 ——天府文化安逸行

Telling Stories of China and Listening to the Voice of Jinjiang —A Pleasant Journey of Tianfu Culture

项目展示与评价 Project Presentation and Evaluation

作品名称 Title of the work	
作品展示 Presentation	（照片粘贴 Stick the photo here）
作品评价 Evaluation	内容维度 Content：☆☆☆☆☆ 形式维度 Form：☆☆☆☆☆

项目感受 Reflection

通过本项目的学习，谈谈你对中国画的了解。

Please talk about your understanding of Chinese painting after learning this project.

第三单元　魅力书画
Unit 3 Charming Calligraphy and Paintings

第三课　趣游锦江，不见不"扇"
—— 荷香墨趣

Be a Fan in Jinjiang
—Lotus in Ink Painting

《捣练图》（局部）
张萱（唐）
Court Ladies Preparing Newly Woven Silk (part)
by Zhang Xuan (Tang Dynasty)

你们知道图中人物拿的是什么吗？

Do you know what the woman in the picture is holding?

中国的团扇。

It's the traditional Chinese circular fan.

它是用来干什么的呢？你知道如何使用它吗？

Do you know what it is used for and how it is used?

103

讲中国故事 听锦江声音——天府文化安逸行

Telling Stories of China and Listening to the Voice of Jinjiang —A Pleasant Journey of Tianfu Culture

今天请大家带上团扇一起去发掘它的用途吧。

Let's explore its usages in our daily life.

项目介绍 Project Introduction

荷塘月色是成都市锦江区人文景观，用于赏荷爱好者近距离观看荷花、欣赏荷花。

Moonlight over the Lotus is a beautiful natural landscape in Jinjiang District, Chengdu. People can take a close look at the beauty and fragrance of lotuses.

荷塘月色
Moonlight over the Lotus

古人3首荷花诗词：

Three ancient poems about lotuses:

小荷才露尖尖角，早有蜻蜓立上头。

A slim lotus leaf, not yet unfurled, scarcely appears;

When on its pointed tip a dragonfly is alighted.

——宋·杨万里《小池》

"A Small Pond" by Yang Wanli, Song Dynasty

第三单元 魅力书画
Unit 3 Charming Calligraphy and Paintings

接天莲叶无穷碧，映日荷花别样红。

Green lotus leaves outspread as far as boundless sky;

Pink lotus blossoms take from sunshine a new dye.

——宋·杨万里《晓出净慈寺送林子方》

"To See off Lin Zifang at Jingci Temple at Dawn"

by Yang Wanli, Song Dynasty

江南可采莲，莲叶何田田。

Let's gather lotus seed by southern river shore!

The lotus sways with teeming leaves we adore.

——汉·汉乐府《江南》

"Gathering Lotus Seeds" in Yuefu, Han Dynasty

(Yuefu poems are Chinese poems composed in a folk song style.)

荷花是我国的传统名花。其花叶清秀，花香四溢，沁人肺腑。有迎骄阳而不惧、出淤泥而不染的气质。

Lotuses are famous in Chinese tradition. Their flowers are beautiful and fragrant, and the leaves are green and elegant. Above all, they stay clean in the dirty soil and stay brave when facing the blazing sun.

中国画家爱画荷花，远有明末清初的八大山人和恽寿平，近有中国画大师吴昌硕、齐白石、张大千等。印象派大师莫奈画了181幅《睡莲》。他们都是画荷花的妙手，每个人对荷花都有自己的刻画和解释。

The Chinese Painters are fond of Painting lotuses, and they can be dated back to late Ming and early Qing Dynasty. The most famous painters include Badashanren (pseudonym of Zhu Da) and Yun Shouping. During modern times, lotuses have been depicted and interpreted not only by several great masters of traditional Chinese painting such as Wu Changshuo, Qi Baishi, and Zhang Daqian, but also by foreign artists. For example, the master of impressionism Oscar-Claude Monet left 181 paintings of lotuses for the world.

讲中国故事 听锦江声音 ——天府文化安逸行
Telling Stories of China and Listening to the Voice of Jinjiang —A Pleasant Journey of Tianfu Culture

✧ 中外名家对比赏析
Compare the two works of lotuses

《睡莲》莫奈
Water Lilies by Monet

《红荷鸳鸯》立轴 齐白石
The Red Lotuses and Mandarin Ducks by Qi Baishi

项目任务 Task

✧ 认识工具
Get to know the tools

1. 文房四宝 Four Treasures of Study
   笔 brush
   墨 ink
   纸 rice paper
   砚 inkstone
2. 印台 ink pad
3. 水拓画工具 Shuita painting kit 
   小棒 stick
   滴管 dropper
   画液 painting liquid
   颜料 Shuita pigment

第三单元　魅力书画
Unit 3 Charming Calligraphy and Paintings

想一想 Think

☆ 让我们试着在诗与画之间，把对荷花的理解画在团扇上。
Let's try to draw the lotus on the fan based on our understanding of the lotus in poems and paintings.

◇ 水拓写意荷花
Draw the lotus in ink painting

1. 调制画液，将颜料摇匀。

Mix the powders to make the liquid for painting and shake them up.

2. 将墨色大胆地滴在画液里，勾勒出荷叶（荷花）的形状，并将图案对印在团扇上。

Drop the ink into the liquid, outline the lotus, and print its shape on the fan.

107

3. 用毛笔进行添画，重墨画出叶脉。

Use the brush with dark ink to draw the leaf vein.

4. 调重墨，添画花瓣、花心、花蕊（以"一点一线"的组合方式描绘）。调淡墨，绘制外侧花瓣，注意外侧完全开放的花瓣墨色应最淡。

Prepare darker ink and draw the petals smoothly. Draw the stamen by connecting the points and the lines. Dip the brush with lighter ink to draw the petals outside. Pay attention to the wide-open petals outside: they should be tinted with the lightest ink.

第三单元　魅力书画
Unit 3 Charming Calligraphy and Paintings

5. 也可以利用海绵添画。

You can also use sponges to paint.

6. 写上自己的姓名和画名，并盖上印章。

Write down your name and the name of your painting, and stamp on it.

项目展示与评价 Project Presentation and Evaluation

作品名称 Title of the work	
作品展示 Presentation	（照片粘贴 Stick the photo here）
作品评价 Evaluation	内容维度 Content：☆☆☆☆☆ 形式维度 Form：☆☆☆☆☆

109

项目感受 Reflection

看到墨彩淋漓的红花墨荷，我们不难联想到诗人杨万里"接天莲叶无穷碧，映日荷花别样红"的诗句。我们于历代诗文中，以荷观物，"爱其清朗闲淡，性所近也"，如梦似幻，自成奇趣！

The red lotus blossoms always remind people of Yang Wanli's poem, "Green lotus leaves outspread as far as boundless sky; Pink lotus blossoms take from sunshine a new dye". In the ancient poems and essays, we view things through lotus, "we love its pureness and indfference to fame and to wealth, and our true virtue is revealed by admiring the lotuses". Sailing in the pond full of lotuses is like a dream, and the lotus is a wonder of its own!

除了可以使用水拓对印之外，我们还可以加入一些其他材料，如家里用的洗衣粉、盐或者是茶叶等，都会让画面上出现神奇的效果。大家可以试一试。

In addition to using ink for printing, we can also use some other materials, such as washing powder, salt or tea, and magical effects will appear on the picture. You can have a try.

说一说：你对中国传统文化有了什么新的认识和了解？

Share with us: what new ideas or insights do you have into Chinese traditional culture?

第三单元　魅力书画
Unit 3 Charming Calligraphy and Paintings

第四课　蜀味年画，情系锦江

Chinese New Year Paintings in Sichuan, a Taste of Jinjiang

你听说过年画吗？

Have you ever heard about Chinese New Year Paintings?

年画？是过年的时候贴的一种画吗？

Chinese New Year Paintings? Are they the paintings put up for the Chinese Lunar New Year?

可以这样说，年画是中国民间习惯在年节张贴的绘画，内容多吉祥喜庆，色彩鲜艳明快。大家快来瞧瞧吧！

You are right! It has been a tradition that we put up Chinese New Year Paintings to celebrate the Spring Festival. These paintings are festive with bright colours. Let's have a look!

讲 中国故事　听 锦江声音　——天府文化安逸行
Telling Stories of China and Listening to the Voice of Jinjiang —A Pleasant Journey of Tianfu Culture

项目介绍　Project Introduction

请大家欣赏这些年画，说一说年画有什么特点？

Please have a look at these Chinese New Year Paintings. Have you found anything special from them?

《门神》
作者　陈方福
Portrait of Door Gods by Chen Fangfu

《海峡两岸合家欢》局部
Part of *Cross-Straits Family Carnival*

《海峡两岸合家欢》局部
Part of *Cross-Straits Family Carnival*

《年画娃娃》
Children in a Chinese New Year Painting

第三单元　魅力书画
Unit 3 Charming Calligraphy and Paintings

✧ 年画的介绍
The introduction of Chinese New Year Paintings

千百年来，年画作为庆祝年节的一种点缀形式，藏着人们对美好的向往，寄托着人们对未来的希望。每逢岁末，很多地方都有张贴年画的习俗，年画表现的是欢乐、美好的事物，寓有吉祥喜庆之意。

For thousands of years, as a kind of decoration to celebrate the festival, Chinese New Year Paintings reveal people's yearning for happiness and their hope for the future. In many places of China, it has become a convention to post the Chinese New Year Paintings at the end of the lunar year. These paintings express joyful and beautiful things, with auspicious and festive meanings.

✧ 年画与我们的生活
Chinese New Year Paintings and our life

过春节贴年画是中国的一种传统习俗。每逢新春佳节，在各大景点、街头巷尾都张贴着许多精美的年画，各地还会举办形式多样的年画活动。

Putting up New Year Paintings on Spring Festival is a tradition in China. During the Spring Festival, many beautiful New Year paintings are posted in scenic spots and streets, and various activities about New Year Paintings are also held in many places.

2002年，绵竹年画被列入中国首批非物质文化遗产名录。2009年，绵竹年画来到了成都市锦江区，随着年画的不断普及和发展，年画吉祥物——"年年""画画"由此诞生了。

In 2002, Mianzhu New Year Paintings was selected as one of the first batch of Chinese intangible cultural heritage list. In 2009, Mianzhu New Year Paintings came to Jinjiang District of Chengdu. With the continuous popularity and development of New Year Paintings, the mascots of New Year Paintings—Niannian and Huahua were born.

那年年和画画都去过成都哪些地方呢？

Where else have Niannian and Huahua been to in Chengdu?

五朵金花 Five Golden Flowers

三圣花乡当然是首要之选，作为成都的新地标，这里是年年和画画向往的小美好。这里花影缤纷，风光旖旎，尤其是那道靓丽的风景线——五朵金花。

Sansheng Flower Town is certainly the priority for you to visit. As an emerging landmark of Chengdu city, it is the paradise that Niannian and Huahua are longing for. Here are colorful flowers and spectacular scenery, especially the Five Golden Flowers, which are renowned for their picturesque and fantastic scenery.

五朵金花？到底是哪"五朵金花"呢？

Five Golden Flowers? What are they?

江家菜地、荷塘月色，是体验艺术魅力的理想之地。

The Jiangs' Vegetable Garden and Moonlight over the Lotus, are ideal places to experience the charm of art.

幸福梅林，因园内遍种梅花而得名，在这

第三单元　魅力书画
Unit 3 Charming Calligraphy and Paintings

里你能了解到梅花与绘画艺术的渊源。

Happy Plum Forest, namely a forest full of plum trees. You can learn about the connection between plum blossoms and the art of painting.

东篱菊园，迎合了现代人返朴归真、回归田园的内心愿望。

Chrysanthemum Garden, catering to modern people's inner desire of returning to the nature.

花乡农居，置身于花海之中的老成都特色农居。

Flowery Farmhouse, a place situated in a sea of flowers with a flavor of old Chengdu.

项目任务 Task

原来年画这么有趣呀，大家想画一画吗？在画之前，我们先来认识一下年画拓印。

They are really interesting! Would you like to have a try? But before we try, let's come and see what materials we need.

完成一幅完整的拓印作品需经过起稿、刷墨、放纸、压平、上色等多道工序。今天，我们一起来体验年画拓印，用

115

到的工具有刻好图案的印版、棕刷、墨汁、盘子、宣纸、粗细不同的毛笔、颜料等。

Creating a frottage of Chinese New Year Painting involves procedures like choosing patterns, brushing ink, placing paper, pressing, and using pigments. Today, we have a chance to create one! The tools we need are printed patterns, coir brushes, ink, an ink plate, rice paper, brushes of various sizes, pigments, etc.

◇ 拓印一幅"门神"年画
Let's make a painting of "Door-God"

（一）准备 Preparation

1. 自由组合四人小组，组长带领组员参观校园年画墙和年画工作室。

Form into groups, with 4 members in ecah group. The team leader leads his/her group to visit the Wall of Chinese New Year Paintings and the art studio.

2. 以小组为单位，选择喜欢的年画印版图案。

Each group chooses their favourite printed pattern.

3. 将棕刷、墨汁、盘子、宣纸、粗细不同的毛笔、颜料等工具备好待用。

Prepare the tools and materials, including coir brushes, ink, an ink plate, rice paper, brushes of various sizes, pigments, etc.

（二）拓印 Frottage

（1）打墨：用棕刷蘸取适量墨汁，以同一方向均匀地将墨打在刻有图案的印版上。

Dip the coir brush in the ink and coat evenly on the board with printed patterns.

第三单元　魅力书画
Unit 3 Charming Calligraphy and Paintings

（2）放纸：将宣纸从中间平铺到刷好墨汁的印版上。

Cover a piece of rice paper on the board from the middle of it.

（3）扫刷：拿出另一个棕刷从中间向四周轻轻地、平整地扫刷，使其均匀地印在纸上。

Get another coir brush and gently brush the paper till it is flat and the pattern is well printed on it.

（4）掀纸：从一侧轻轻地掀开宣纸，等待墨干。

Remove the paper from one side very carefully and wait until the ink gets dry.

（5）着色：选用适当的颜色进行着色，完成作品。

Paint with colours accordingly. Your painting is completed.

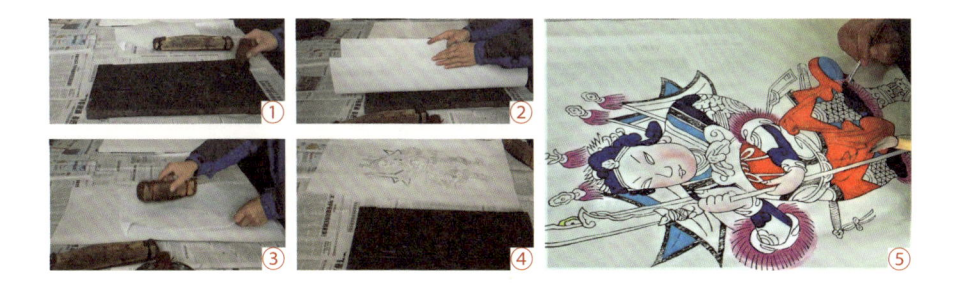

项目展示与评价 Project Presentation and Evaluation

作品名称 Title of the work	
作品展示 Presentation	（照片粘贴 Stick the photo here）

117

讲中国故事 听锦江声音——天府文化安逸行
Telling Stories of China and Listening to the Voice of Jinjiang —A Pleasant Journey of Tianfu Culture

| 作品评价
Evaluation | 内容维度 Content：☆☆☆☆☆

形式维度 Form：☆☆☆☆☆ |

项目感受 Reflection

通过本项目的学习，你对中国传统文化年画有新的认识吗？

Through the learning of this project, do you have any new understanding of Chinese New Year Paintings as a traditional culture?

第三单元　魅力书画
Unit 3 Charming Calligraphy and Paintings

第五课　锦江晒冬阳，好柿画成双

Bathe in Winter Sunshine and Draw Persimmons in Pairs

欢迎来到中国画课堂。

Welcome to our traditional Chinese painting class.

中国画是什么？

What is traditional Chinese painting?

中国画的文化源远流长，它蕴含了中国几千年的艺术灵魂和文人思想。

With a history dating back to thousands of years ago, Chinese painting embodies the essence of traditional Chinese art and the values of Chinese artists.

今天我们就要用这些材料来画画吗？

Are we going to use these tools and materials in our painting class today?

119

讲中国故事 听锦江声音 ——天府文化安逸行
Telling Stories of China and Listening to the Voice of Jinjiang —A Pleasant Journey of Tianfu Culture

我们会用到这些工具，它们分别是笔、墨、纸、砚。

Yes. We will use a Chinese calligraphy brush pen, ink, a piece of rice paper and an inkstone.

这些果子是什么呀？能吃么？

What are these? Are they edible?

这些是柿子，一种好吃的水果。柿子的原产地在中国。已有上千年栽培史的柿子，因"柿"谐音"事"，中国人便将诸多喜庆吉祥的内涵融入其中，如"事事如意""四世同堂""事事安顺""事事有余"等。

These are persimmons, a kind of delicious fruit originated in China thousands of years ago. In Chinese, persimmon is pronounced as "Shi" (柿), which is homophonic to "Shi" (事) meaning "things" or "Shi" (世) meaning "generations". For this reason, persimmon has many auspicious connotations. For example, when we say "Shi Shi Ru Yi" (事事如意), we hope that everything goes well in our life. "Si Shi Tong Tang" (四世同堂) signifies a large family with four generations living together. "Shi Shi An Shun" (事事安顺) suggests that everything is fine. "Shi Shi You Yu" (事事有余) symbolizes abundance.

项目介绍 Project Introduction

◇ **柿子与西红柿**

Persimmon and tomato

柿子看起来有点像西红柿，但是又有些不一样，味道也不同。

Though similar to tomato in appearance, persimmon is different from tomato in other ways.

西红柿
Tomato

柿子
Persimmon

1. 科属不同 Different classification

西红柿是管状花目、茄科、番茄属的一种一年生或多年生草本植物，柿子是柿科、柿属植物，落叶乔木，原产于东亚地区。

Belonging to the order Tubiflorae and classified as Solanaceae and the genus Solanum, tomato is an annual or perennial herbaceous plant. In contrast, as a plant of the genus Diospyros, persimmon is a deciduous tree native to East Asia.

2. 分布不同 Different distribution

西红柿原产南美洲，在中国南北方广泛栽培。柿子原产我国长江流域，各省、区多有栽培。在朝鲜、日本、东南亚、大洋洲等也有栽培。

Although native to South America, tomatoes are widely cultivated in the north and south of China. In contrast, originating in China's Yangtze River basin, persimmons are planted in many provinces and regions of China as well as in North Korea, Japan, Southeast Asia, Oceania, etc.

3. 生长环境不同 Different environment

西红柿是一种喜温性的蔬菜，喜光，喜水。柿树是深根性树种，又是阳性树种。

Tomato is a thermophilic and hygrophilous plant that often thrives under sunlight, while persimmon is a heliophilous tree species that has deep roots.

项目任务 Task

◆ 绘画
Painting

1. 用狼毫毛笔调朱磦色，并一笔画出柿子的上半部分。

Use a Chinese writing brush made of weasel's hair to draw the upper part of the persimmon with red color in one stroke.

2. 顺着柿子的弧度画出下半部分。

Draw the lower half along the upper part of the persimmon.

3. 用重墨点果蒂。

Use some black ink to draw the pedicel.

第三单元　魅力书画
Unit 3 Charming Calligraphy and Paintings

4. 用花青色加藤黄色调出墨绿色，左右两笔画叶子，并用浓墨勾叶脉。

Mix cyan and gamboge to create blackish green. Then paint leaves in two stokes on the left and right side respectively, and delineate the leaf veins in blackish green.

5. 整组的柿子最好有遮挡变化，树枝应画得较硬朗。

A group of persimmons should better appear layered, and the branches should be painted with hard lines.

◇ 题字（写上画名和自己的姓名）

Inscription (write down your name and the name of the painting on the paper)

两个柿子，代表好事成双，好的运气一起到来。

Persimmons in pairs signify that good things will come in pairs.

123

讲 中国故事 听 锦江声音 ——天府文化安逸行
Telling Stories of China and Listening to the Voice of Jinjiang —A Pleasant Journey of Tianfu Culture

项目展示与评价 Project Presentation and Evaluation

作品名称 Title of the work	
作品展示 Presentation	（照片粘贴 Stick the photo here）
作品评价 Evaluation	内容维度 Content：☆☆☆☆☆ 形式维度 Form：☆☆☆☆☆

项目感受 Reflection

说一说：你对中国传统文化或者中国画有了什么新的认识和了解？

Share with us: what new insights have you gained into traditional Chinese culture or Chinese painting?

第三单元　魅力书画

Unit 3 Charming Calligraphy and Paintings

第六课　夏日绵长，好"竹"意

Through Bamboo, Enjoy Chinese Culture

你能猜猜这是什么吗？

Can you guess what it is?

左边一个，右边一个，熊猫见了，心里快乐。

One on the left and one on the right; a panda sees it and feels happy inside.

难道是竹子？

Is it bamboo?

对啦，就是竹子。它是世界上生长最快的植物，有些竹子每天可长40厘米。竹子的用途也特别多，它能做成竹篮、竹椅、筷子、凉席、衣服等。下面我们一起去了解一下竹子吧！

Yes, it's bamboo. It is the fastest growing plant in the world. Some bamboos can grow 40 cm per day. Bamboo has many uses. It can be made into baskets, chairs, chopsticks, summer sleeping mats, and clothes. Let's learn more about bamboo!

讲中国故事 听锦江声音 ——天府文化安逸行
Telling Stories of China and Listening to the Voice of Jinjiang —A Pleasant Journey of Tianfu Culture

项目介绍 Project Introduction

✧ **竹子的特征**
The characteristics of bamboo

竹与梅、兰、菊并称为"花中四君子",与梅、松并称为"岁寒三友",很多竹子的原产地在中国。从古至今的文人墨客中,爱竹咏竹者众多。

Bamboo, plum, orchid and chrysanthemum are called "Four Gentlemen of Flowers" since they are regarded as a symbol of integrity just like gentlemen. Also, there is "Three Friends in Cold Weather" to describe bamboo, plum and pine, which are three durable plants in winter. Many varieties of bamboos originate in China, from ancient times till now, there are many men of letters who love bamboo and write poems in praise of it.

✧ **竹子与我们的生活**
Bamboo and our life

竹子可用于制作工艺品、乐器等。除此之外,竹子还可被用作纺织品，做成毛巾和衣物等。将竹材通过烘培制成的竹炭，也有许多用途，如去除环境中的气味。生活中常见的扫帚、竹椅、箩筐、背篓、席子等也是由竹子制成的。

Bamboo can be used to make handicrafts and musical instruments. Besides, it can be used as textiles to produce towels and clothes. Bamboo is also baked to make bamboo charcoal, which is used in many ways, such as removing odors in the environment. Common items like brooms, chairs, baskets, and mats are also made of bamboo.

在成都有一个以竹闻名的公园，叫望江楼公园，位于锦江畔，是以竹为主的园林，也是全国竹子品种最多的专类公园。园内荟萃了四百多种竹子。竹的神韵、价值和精神都在这里尽数体现。

In Chengdu, there is a park famous for bamboo called Wangjiang Pavilion Park, which is located on the bank of Jinjiang River. This is a theme park of bamboo culture with the largest variety of bamboos in China, gathering more than 400 kinds of bamboos. The charm, value, and spirit of bamboo are fully reflected here.

项目任务 Task

◇ 品味竹意
Learn the implication

一、读一读 Read

1. 和老师合作读一读《竹子谣》。

Please read *Bamboo Ballad* together with your teacher.

2. 尝试用四川话读一读《竹子谣》。

Please try to read *Bamboo Ballad* in Sichuan dialect.

青竹子，
紫竹子，
圆竹子，
方竹子，
竹子做成竹屋子，
竹屋里住着竹鸡子，
竹鸡吃着竹虫子，
竹虫要吃竹叶子，
竹叶连着竹枝子，
竹枝连着竹节子。

Green bamboo,

Purple bamboo,

Round bamboo,

Square bamboo.

Bamboo is made into a bamboo house.

Bamboo chickens live in the bamboo house.

Bamboo chickens eat bamboo worms.

Bamboo worms want to eat bamboo leaves.

Bamboo leaves are connected to bamboo branches.

Bamboo branches connect with bamboo knots.

第三单元　魅力书画
Unit 3 Charming Calligraphy and Paintings

✧ 感受竹韵
Feel the charm

二、诵一诵 Recite

吟诵《竹石》，感悟竹子的精神。

Please recite the poem "Bamboo and Rock", and feel the spirit of bamboo.

竹　石

（清）郑板桥

咬定青山不放松，立根原在破岩中。
千磨万击还坚劲，任尔东西南北风。

Bamboo and Rock

by Zheng Banqiao (Qing Dynasty)

Between broken rocks striking my root deep,

I hold the mountain green and won't let go.

From whichever direction the winds leap,

I remain strong, though facing many a blow.

✧ 体验竹趣
Have some fun

三、画一画 Draw

1. 准备。准备大小不一的竹筒（已洗净晾干并分类）、颜料、棉签、画笔。

Preparing. Prepare bamboo tubes of different sizes (washed, dried and classified), pigments, cotton swabs, and brushes.

2. 起型。用铅笔画好草稿，确定图案的位置。

Drafting. Draw a draft with a pencil and locate the pattern.

3. 上色。先铺大色调，观察好整体色调和色彩关系后，尽快薄涂。淡淡地铺第一遍底色，注意色彩的搭配。

Coloring. Paint the major colors first. Observe and confirm the overall tones and colors, and paint thinly as soon as possible. Spread the background color lightly for the first time, and pay attention to color matching.

4. 画细节。比第一遍画得更厚一些，并添加装饰，深入刻画细节。

Drawing details. Draw on the first layer of color, add decorations and depict details in depth.

5. 整体观察。调整并进行最后的修饰。

Observing. Observe if there is anything that needs modifying and make the final changes.

项目展示与评价 Project Presentation and Evaluation

作品名称 Title of the work	
作品展示 Presentation	（照片粘贴 Stick the photo here）

第三单元　魅力书画

Unit 3 Charming Calligraphy and Paintings

作品评价 Evaluation	内容维度 Content：☆☆☆☆☆
	形式维度 Form：☆☆☆☆☆

项目感受 Reflection

通过今天的学习体验，你觉得最大的收获是什么？请你谈谈自己的感受。

What have you learned through today's learning? Please talk about your feelings.

第四单元 成都美食
Unit 4 Chengdu Tasty Foods

第四单元　成都美食
Unit 4 Chengdu Tasty Foods

第一课　唤起记忆中的甜 —— 成都糖画

Refresh the Memory of Sweetness
—Chengdu Sugar Painting

你品尝过成都糖画吗？

Have you ever tasted Chengdu sugar painting?

糖画？可以品尝，那它不是画而是糖吗？

Sugar painting? I'd like to have a try, so it's not a painting but sugar. Am I right?

可以这样说，糖画是一种传统民间手工艺，是以糖为材料来进行造型的。大家来尝尝吧！

It can be said that sugar painting is a kind of traditional folk handicraft, which uses sugar as the material to make different shapes. Please have a try!

135

讲中国故事 听锦江声音 ——天府文化安逸行
Telling Stories of China and Listening to the Voice of Jinjiang —A Pleasant Journey of Tianfu Culture

项目介绍 Project Introduction

请大家欣赏这些糖画，说一说这些糖画都是什么图案。
Please look at these sugar paintings and say what patterns they are.

蝴蝶 Butterfly

螃蟹 Crab

孔雀 Peacock

孙悟空 Sun Wukong

小猪佩奇 Peppa Pig

大刀 Machete

第四单元　成都美食
Unit 4 Chengdu Tasty Foods

熊猫 Panda　　　　　　　　　鹿 Deer

✧ 糖画的介绍
The introduction of sugar painting

　　成都糖画，过去又称"倒糖饼儿""糖粑粑儿"等，是用融化的糖汁作画的一种手工技艺，主要流传于成都市及其周边地区。它也是一种既能品尝又能观赏的传统工艺品，距今已有400多年的历史。

　　In the past, Chengdu sugar painting was also called "sugar cake", "sugar bread" and so on. It is a craft of painting with melted sugar, and it is popular in Chengdu and its surrounding areas. It is also a traditional handicraft that can be both tasted and appreciated, and has a history of more than 400 years.

　　糖画是中国民俗文化的重要组成，反映了古时人们的思想和生活场景等。它作为民间文化传承的载体，经过长时间的发展演变，借鉴了各种造型手法和技艺，融合了各种民间艺术的创作思路和技巧，如剪纸、雕刻、皮影、书法等，把神话人物、民俗场景、飞鸟走兽、戏剧角色等富有吉祥意味的图案展现出来，为人们的文化生活增添亮丽的色彩，满足了人们的审美需求。它蕴含着形态万千的中国元素，生动地展现出人们对生活的热爱和对甜蜜生活的向往。

　　Sugar painting plays an important part in Chinese folk culture, and it reflects ancient people's thoughts and life scenes. As one of the carriers of folk cultural heritage and after a long development, it learns from all sorts of modelling methods and techniques, integrates creative thinking and skills of folk art, such as paper cutting, carving, shadow play, and calligraphy, and displays auspicious patterns of mythological figures, folk scenes, birds, animals and dramatic characters, which add bright colors to people's cultural life and meet people's aesthetic needs. It contains various Chinese elements and vividly shows people's love and yearning for sweet life.

✧ **糖画与我们的生活**
Sugar painting and our life

1993年，成都市锦江区被文化部授予"民间糖画艺术之乡"的称号。2008年，成都糖画入选我国第二批国家级非物质文化遗产保护项目名录。可以说，糖画与我们锦江区的联系非常密切。

In 1993, Jinjiang District of Chengdu was awarded the "Hometown of Folk Sugar Painting Art" by the Ministry of Culture. In 2008, Chengdu Sugar Painting was selected into the second batch of national intangible cultural heritage protection list in China. It can be said that sugar painting is closely related to Jinjiang District.

在成都各大景点、各个休闲公园、街头巷尾都能看见糖画摊。在锦江的著名景点，如春熙路、塔子山公园、三圣花乡等地，都能看到糖画摊前簇拥着很多游客。

Sugar painting stalls can be found in scenic spots, leisure parks and streets in Chengdu. At famous scenic spots, such as Chunxi Road, Tazishan Park, and Sansheng Flower Town, you can see many tourists crowding around sugar painting stalls.

第四单元　成都美食
Unit 4 Chengdu Tasty Foods

项目任务 Task

　　这么好吃好玩的糖画，大家想要尝试制作吗？首先，我们来认识一下制作工具。

　　What delicious and interesting sugar paintings they are! Do you want to have a try? First, let's take a look at the tools.

转盘 Turntable

大理石板、刷子、起子、刀、勺、锅
Marble slab, brush, shovel, knife, spoon, pot

◇ 制作一个简单的糖画"桃子"

Let's make a simple sugar painting of "peach"

139

讲 中国故事　听 锦江声音　——天府文化安逸行

Telling Stories of China and Listening to the Voice of Jinjiang —A Pleasant Journey of Tianfu Culture

一、准备 Preparation

1. 对操作台面进行消毒。

Disinfect the operation table.

2. 将油壶中的清油均匀、少量地喷至操作台面。

Evenly spray a small amount of edible vegetable oil from the oil pot to the operation table.

3. 将准备好的糖块小火熬制成拉丝状。

Boil the prepared sugar cubes over low heat until it gets ropy.

二、制作 Production

1. 用"按头子"和"拭皮子"的方式完成桃子的两片叶子。

Paint the two leaves by means of "Antouzi" (pressing skillfully while the liquid sugar is warm) and "Shipizi" (wiping artistically to make the basic patterns).

第四单元　成都美食
Unit 4 Chengdu Tasty Foods

2. 用拉丝的方式完成桃子果实外轮廓的勾勒。

Complete the outline of peach by stretching.

3. 用拉丝的方式绘制果实内部。

Draw the inside of the fruit by stretching.

4. 在糖画中央粘上竹签固定。

Stick the bamboo stick in the middle of the sugar painting.

中国故事 听 锦江声音 ——天府文化安逸行
Telling Stories of China and Listening to the Voice of Jinjiang —A Pleasant Journey of Tianfu Culture

项目展示与评价 Project Presentation and Evaluation

作品名称 Title of the work	
作品展示 Presentation	（照片粘贴 Stick the photo here）
作品评价 Evaluation	内容维度 Content：☆☆☆☆☆ 形式维度 Form：☆☆☆☆☆

项目感受 Reflection

通过本项目的学习，根据你对糖画的了解，谈谈你眼里的成都。

Through the study of this project, please talk about Chengdu in your eyes based on your understanding of sugar painting.

第四单元　成都美食
Unit 4 Chengdu Tasty Foods

第二课　"锦锦"有味，"蜀"你最甜
—— 超甜的糖油果子

Super Sweet Snack in Jinjiang, Sichuan
—Tangyou Guozi

最近我读到了一首打油诗："包糖胜过汤麻饼，不见青青陌上桑。"这写的是我喜欢的一种成都名小吃，你猜猜是什么？
I read a ragged verse recently. It said: "Sugar-coated rice balls are much more tasty than Tang's Sesame Cookies, and you do not care about the beauty under the mulberry tree." It refers to a famous Chengdu snack that I like very much. Can you guess what's that?

让我想一想……我猜不出来，是什么呀？
Let me see. I have no idea. What's that?

这是成都非常有名的小吃之一——糖油果子，其特点是色泽黄亮、外酥内糯、香甜可口，非常好吃。
It's one of the famous local snacks in Chengdu—Tangyou Guozi. It is characterized by its brown and bright color, and its crispy outside while soft and sticky inside. It's very sweet and yummy.

143

讲 中国故事　听 锦江声音　——天府文化安逸行
Telling Stories of China and Listening to the Voice of Jinjiang —A Pleasant Journey of Tianfu Culture

"包糖胜过汤麻饼",真的很形象!好想来一串!
"Sugar-coated rice balls are much more tasty than Tang's Sesame Cookies." It's really vivid! I do want to have a taste!

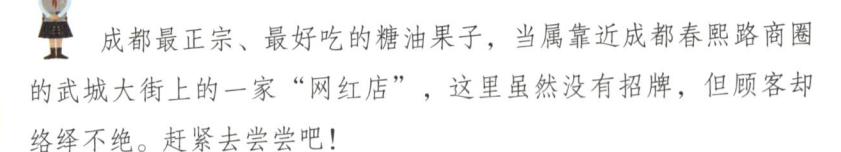

成都最正宗、最好吃的糖油果子,当属靠近成都春熙路商圈的武城大街上的一家"网红店",这里虽然没有招牌,但顾客却络绎不绝。赶紧去尝尝吧!
The most tasty and famous Tangyou Guozi in Chengdu is sold in a trending store online located on Wucheng Street near the Chunxi Road bussiness center. Although it has no signboard, there are customers coming and going in succession. Let's go and have a try!

项目介绍　Project Introduction

◇ 糖油果子的历史
The history of Tangyou Guozi

糖油果子,又叫"天鹅蛋"(因形似而得名),是成都著名的小吃,和荞面、肥肠粉合称"青石桥三绝"。

Tangyou Guozi, also called "Swan Egg" (for its similar shape), is a famous local snack in Chengdu. Together with buckwheat noodles and rice noodles, they are called the "Three delicious snacks in Qingshiqiao".

第四单元 成都美食
Unit 4 Chengdu Tasty Foods

糖油果子至今大概有一千多年的历史，可以追溯到唐宋时期，当时叫"焦（jiāo）䭔（duī）"，其味甜皮脆，酥香内软而不腻。唐代著名的白话诗爱好者王梵志和尚也有一句诗"贪他油煎䭔，爱若菠萝蜜"，形容的就是糖油果子。皮脆香甜的糖油果子朴实又美味，焦脆的外皮带着红糖的甜味，嚼着除了糯米香还有芝麻粒的香味，简直是人间美味。

It has a history of more than 1000 years. In ancient Tang and Song Dynasty, Tangyou Guozi was called "Jiao Dui". It is sweet and crispy outside, and soft but not greasy inside. Wang Fanzhi, a well-known vernacular poet in Tang Dynasty said in a poem that "greedy for Jiao Dui, sweet as much as jackfruit", which described Tangyou Guozi. Its crispy crust is coated with sweet brown sugar, and the combined flavor of sticky rice and sesame makes it perfect.

糖油果子旧时在成都花会上最盛行，许多人都拿着用竹签串着的糖油果子边吃边走，赏花看灯，形成了花会上又一饮食景观。糖油果子以串售卖，一串为四到五个，现在在成都的小巷里、庙会上仍能找到。

Tangyou Guozi was most popular at Chengdu Flower Fair in the old days. Many people walked with a bunch of Tangyou Guozi while watching the beautiful flowers and the lanterns, which forms a special landscape at the flower fair. Tangyou Guozi is sold in a bunch, which has four to five fried rice balls . Now it can still be found in alleys and temple fairs in Chengdu.

项目任务 Task

这么美味的糖油果子，大家想要试着做一串吗？
Tangyou Guozi is so delicious. Why not make a bunch of it by ourselves?

✧ 制作一串糖油果子
Let's make a bunch of Tangyou Guozi

Telling Stories of China and Listening to the Voice of Jinjiang —A Pleasant Journey of Tianfu Culture

首先，我们来认识一下需要用到的材料。

First, let's see what ingredients are needed.

材料：
- 糯米粉100克
- 红糖30克
- 白糖25克
- 大米粉20克
- 温水85克
- 食用油适量
- 熟白芝麻适量

Ingredients:
- 100g glutinous rice flour
- 30g brown sugar
- 25g white sugar
- 20g rice flour
- 85g warm water
- cooking oil
- fried white sesame

第一步：将糯米粉、大米粉和白糖放入容器中，混合均匀。

Step 1: Put glutinous rice flour, rice flour and white sugar into the container and mix them well.

第二步：倒入温水，边倒边搅拌，和成面团。

Step 2: Pour the right amount of warm water into the container, and stir them while pouring. Knead them into a dough.

第三步：将面团分为约15克一个的剂子并搓圆，放在纱布上备用。

Step 3: Divide the dough into small parts, and each part is about 15 grams. Make them round like small balls and put them on the gauze.

第四步：在锅中按照3比1的比例先后放入没有加热的冷油和切碎的红糖。

Step 4: Put the unheated oil and chopped brown sugar in the pot at a ratio of 3∶1.

第五步：开中小火将红糖烧化，等红

第四单元　成都美食

Unit 4 Chengdu Tasty Foods

糖全部浮上来后关火。

Step 5: Turn on small heat to melt the brown sugar. Turn off the heat when the brown sugar comes up.

第六步：放置片刻，等油温稍微降下来，红糖沉入油底。

Step 6: Let the oil cool down and wait until the brown sugar sinks into the bottom of the oil.

第七步：依次放入圆子，开小火慢炸。注意不要马上搅动，可以轻轻晃动锅。炸一会后，如果有粘连，可以用筷子轻轻将它们分开，并在锅里划动，使其受热均匀。

Step 7: Turn on small heat and fry the rice balls one by one. Do not stir them right away, instead you can move the pot gently. After a while, you can use chopsticks to separate the sticky rice balls and stir gently to make sure that they are heated evenly.

第八步：一两分钟后，用勺子来回推动，直到上色均匀、外壳变硬，呈现糖浆色即可关火。

Step 8: After one minute or two, stir the rice balls back and forth with a spoon to make sure they are coated well by brown sugar. Turn off the heat when the outside becomes crispy and brown.

第九步：捞出后趁热撒入熟白芝麻，拌匀后插上竹签即可。趁热吃风味更佳。

Step 9: Sprinkle white sesame around the balls while they are hot, and then skewer them with a bamboo stick. Enjoy them while they are warm.

讲 中国故事 听 锦江声音 ——天府文化安逸行
Telling Stories of China and Listening to the Voice of Jinjiang —A Pleasant Journey of Tianfu Culture

项目展示与评价 Project Presentation and Evaluation

作品名称 Title of the work	
作品展示 Presentation	（照片粘贴 Stick the photo here）
作品评价 Evaluation	内容维度 Content：☆☆☆☆☆ 形式维度 Form：☆☆☆☆☆

项目感受 Reflection

糖油果子是成都人舌尖上的一味甜蜜记忆。亲手制作并品尝了糖油果子后，你是否也有这种甜蜜的感受呢？和同伴交流一下吧。

For the local people in Chengdu, Tangyou Guozi is a sweet memory on the tip of the tongue. After making and tasting Tangyou Gouzi by yourself, do you have the same sweet feelings as well? Please share with your partners.

第四单元　成都美食
Unit 4 Chengdu Tasty Foods

第三课　"锦锦"乐道，深"馅"其中
——鲜美的龙抄手

Famous Snack with Heavy and Tasty Fillings
—Delicious Long Chaoshou

"西蜀名肴如集锦，老饕不厌百回尝"，你知道我说的是成都哪种有名的小吃吗？

"Although there are many famous delicacies in West Shu, it can be a favorite for you." Do you know what kind of famous Chengdu snacks I'm talking about?

成都有名的小吃太多啦，我一时猜不出来。

There are too many famous snacks in Chengdu. I can't figure it out.

这是外地人来成都必打卡的美食之一"龙抄手"。

It's Long Chaoshou, the wontons, a snack that visitors must enjoy in Chengdu.

那一定很好吃吧！要在哪里才能吃到最正宗的龙抄手呢？

It must be delicious. Where can I find the most authentic Long Chaoshou?

149

讲中国故事 听锦江声音——天府文化安逸行
Telling Stories of China and Listening to the Voice of Jinjiang —A Pleasant Journey of Tianfu Culture

当然是在大名鼎鼎的"龙抄手"春熙路总店啦，这里的龙抄手皮薄、馅嫩、汤鲜，还有原汤、酸辣等各种不同口味。真是令人赞不绝口，我们赶紧去尝尝吧！

You'd better go to the famous "Long Chaoshou" headquarters in Chunxi Road. The wontons offered by the restaurant are praised for their thin wrappers, tender meat fillings and fresh soup. It has various flavors: the original taste, sour and hot taste, and so on. It tastes so good. Let's have a try!

项目介绍 Project Introduction

✧ 龙抄手的历史
The history of Long Chaoshou

龙抄手皮薄馅嫩，爽滑鲜香，汤浓色白，为蓉城小吃店铺的佼佼者。

Long Chaoshou is famous for its thin wrappers, tender and smooth fillings, as well as thick and white soup. It is one of the best snacks in

第四单元　成都美食
Unit 4 Chengdu Tasty Foods

Chengdu.

龙抄手的得名并非老板姓龙，而是创办人张武光与其好友在当时的"浓花茶园"商议开抄手店之事，在讨论店名时，借用"浓花茶园"的"浓"字，以谐音字"龙"为名号（四川方言中"浓"与"龙"同音），也寓有"龙腾虎跃""吉祥""生意兴隆"之意。

Long Chaoshou got its name not because the founder's surname was "Long". In fact, when Zhang Wuguang, the founder of Long Chaoshou, and his three friends discussed the plan to establish a wonton restaurant, they gathered at a teahouse named "Nong Hua Teahouse". Since in Sichuan dialect, the pronunciation of "Long" (龙) and "Nong" (浓) are the same. And "Long" in Chinese means good fortune and booming business. That's why they used "Long" as the name of their shop.

"抄手"是四川人对馄饨的特殊叫法，抄手的得名大概是因为包制时要将面皮的两头抄拢。

"Chaoshou" is a unique way Sichuan people refer to wontons, and it literally means making wontons in the shape of folded hands.

成都的"龙抄手"于1941年开设于成都的悦来场，20世纪50年代初迁往新集场，60年代后又迁至锦江区春熙路南段至今，迄今已有70余年的历史。

"Long Chaoshou" was founded in Yuelai Market in Chengdu in 1941. It moved to a new market in the early 1950s, and to the southern section of Chunxi Road in Jinjiang District During 1960s. It has been more than 70 years since then.

项目任务 Task

这么美味的龙抄手，相信你也迫不及待地想要自己尝试做一碗吧！

Long Chaoshou is so delicious. I believe you can't wait to make a bowl of them by yourself.

讲中国故事 听锦江声音 ——天府文化安逸行
Telling Stories of China and Listening to the Voice of Jinjiang —A Pleasant Journey of Tianfu Culture

◆ 制作一碗龙抄手

Let's make a bowl of Long Chaoshou

首先，我们来认识一下需要用到的材料。

First, let's see what ingredients are needed.

材料：	**Ingredients:**
● 猪肉200g	● 200g pork
● 面粉150g	● 150g flour
● 鸡蛋一个	● an egg
● 葱20g	● 20g green onion
● 盐适量	● salt
● 味精适量	● gourmet powder
● 胡椒粉适量	● pepper
● 酱油适量	● soy sauce
● 芝麻油适量	● sesame oil

第一步：将肥三瘦七比例的猪肉用刀背捶茸去筋，剁细成泥，加入盐、酱油、香油搅打（若觉得肉馅干的话，可以边搅拌边加入些清水），然后放入葱末，搅成干糊状并拌匀，制成馅料备用。

Step 1: Choose the pork of a perfect lean-to-fat ratio of seven to three. Use the back of a knife to chop the pork and remove the tendons, and then make it into mince. Add proper amount of salt, soy sauce, and sesame oil, and stir them together (if the meat is dry, you can add some water while stirring). Add the chopped green onions, stir and mix them well into a dry paste. That's the meat fillings.

第四单元　成都美食

Unit 4 Chengdu Tasty Foods

第二步：把面粉放在案板上，放盐少许，磕入鸡蛋1个，再加清水调匀，揉和成面团，面不要太软。面和成面团后饧20分钟。

Step 2: Put flour on the chopping board, then add a little salt, an egg and some water, and mix them well. Knead it into a dough, which should not be too soft. Then leave the dough aside for about 20 minutes.

第三步：饧好后，用擀面杖将面团擀成纸一样薄的面片。

Step 3: Use a rolling pin to make the dough into paper-thin slices.

第四步：折好后，切四指见方的方形抄手皮备用。

Step 4: Fold the slices, and cut them into square wrappers as wide as four fingers.

第五步：取一张抄手皮，在面片中放入适量的馅料。

Step 5: Take a piece of wrapper and put an appropriate amount of meat fillings on it.

第六步：对角折成三角形。

Step 6: Fold it diagonally into a triangle.

讲 中国故事 **听** 锦江声音 ——天府文化安逸行
Telling Stories of China and Listening to the Voice of Jinjiang —A Pleasant Journey of Tianfu Culture

第七步：再把左右角向中间叠起并粘在一起，做成长菱形抄手坯。

Step 7: Fold the left and right corners to the middle and stick them together. A diamond-shaped wonton is made.

第八步：锅中烧开水，下入抄手，将其煮熟，火候要恰到好处。注意不要煮太久，不然馅容易漏出。

Step 8: Boil some water in the pot. Put wontons into the boiling water and cook them well. Be careful not to cook for a long time since the meat fillings is easy to get out.

第九步：碗内盛入原汤，加盐、味精、胡椒粉、芝麻油、葱花兑制成汤，再放入煮熟的抄手即成。

Step 9: Put clear soup made from chicken, duck and pork in the bowl. Add salt, gourmet powder, pepper, sesame oil, and chopped green onions together, and then put the well-cooked wontons into the bowl. Your Long Chaoshou is ready.

第四单元　成都美食

Unit 4 Chengdu Tasty Foods

项目展示与评价 Project Presentation and Evaluation

作品名称 Title of the work	
作品展示 Presentation	（照片粘贴 Stick the photo here）
作品评价 Evaluation	内容维度 Content：☆☆☆☆☆ 形式维度 Form：☆☆☆☆☆

项目感受 Reflection

　　有着百年历史的龙抄手，制作工艺十分讲究，每一步都要认真完成，每一枚抄手都厚实饱满，吃在嘴里细嫩鲜美，再来一口原汤，实在是满足。怎么样？你对自己制作的龙抄手还满意吗？交流一下你的看法吧！

　　Long Chaoshou with a history of a hundred years is also noted for its exquisite craftsmanship. Every step must be carefully completed. Each wonton is plump and full of meat, which tastes tender and delicious. Also, drinking the clear soup makes you satisfied. How about your Long Chaoshou? Are you satisfied with the wontons made by yourself? Share your opinions with your partners!

第四课　甜甜蜜蜜话团圆
——成都名小吃"赖汤圆"

Tales of Happy Reunion
—Chengdu Famous Snack "Lai Tangyuan"

你听过这首歌吗？"卖汤圆，卖汤圆，小二哥的汤圆是圆又圆！"

Have you heard this song before? "Tangyuan, Tangyuan, the little brother's Tangyuan is round and round!"

我当然听过，我们成都的赖汤圆也是又圆又甜！

Of course. "Lai Tangyuan" of Chengdu is round and sweet!

对！这是成都的名小吃。

Yes. It's one of the most famous snacks in Chengdu.

哇！真的很有特色！不知道哪里能吃到呢？

Wow! It's really special! Where can we have it?

第四单元　成都美食

Unit 4 Chengdu Tasty Foods

> 在锦江区总府路的赖汤圆美食店，就能尝到正宗的赖汤圆！
>
> You can taste the most authentic Lai Tangyuan in Chengdu at the Lai Tangyuan food shop, which is located at Zongfu Road of Jinjiang District.

项目介绍 Project Introduction

✧ 赖汤圆的历史
The history of Lai Tangyuan

赖汤圆创始于1894年，创制人名叫赖元鑫。由于父病母亡，赖元鑫跟着堂兄来到成都挑起担子卖汤圆，直至30年代才在总府街口买了间铺面，坐店经营，取名"赖汤圆"。他的汤圆选料精、做工细、质优价廉、细腻柔和、皮薄馅丰、软糯香甜。有煮时不浑汤，吃时"三不粘"（不粘筷、不粘碗、不粘牙）的特点。上桌时，一碗四个，四种馅心，小巧玲珑。

Lai Tangyuan was established in 1894 by Lai Yuanxin. Since his father was sick and his mother passed away, Lai Yuanxin followed his cousin to Chengdu and sold tangyuan by the road. After years of hard work, he started a shop named "Lai Tangyuan" at the corner of Zongfu Road. His tangyuan is made of fine materials with thin and soft skin and rich filling, and it is of high quality and reasonable price. While cooking, the tangyuan soup is clear. While eating, the tangyuan doesn't stick chopsticks, bowls or teeth. There are 4 tangyuan in each bowl with different fillings. They are small and exquisite.

讲中国故事 听锦江声音 ——天府文化安逸行
Telling Stories of China and Listening to the Voice of Jinjiang —A Pleasant Journey of Tianfu Culture

项目任务 Task

你想尝试做一碗赖汤圆吗？

Do you want to try making a bowl of Lai Tangyuan?

制作一碗赖汤圆
Make a bowl of Lai Tangyuan

首先，我们来认识一下需要用到的材料。

First, let's see what ingredients are needed.

用料：
- 糯米500克
- 大米75克
- 黑芝麻70克
- 白糖粉300克
- 面粉50克
- 板化油200克
- 白糖及麻酱各适量

Ingredients:
- 500g glutinous rice
- 75g rice
- 70g black sesame
- 300g white sugar flour
- 50g flour
- 200g lard
- some sugar and sesame paste

第一步：将糯米、大米淘洗干净，浸泡48小时，再清洗一次。加入适量清水磨成稀浆，装入布袋内，吊干成汤圆面。现在超市有现成的汤圆粉。

Step1: Wash the glutinous rice and rice, dip them in water for 48 hours, and then wash again. Add some water and grind it to thin paste. Put it in a cloth bag, and hang dry into tangyuan flour. You can buy it in the supermarket nowadays.

第二步：将芝麻去杂质，淘洗干净，用小火炒熟、炒香，用擀面杖压成细面，加入糖粉、面粉、化猪油，揉拌均匀，置于案板上压紧。现

第四单元　成都美食

Unit 4 Chengdu Tasty Foods

在超市有现成的汤圆馅。

Sept 2: Remove impurities among the sesame, wash it and then fry it over low heat. After frying, use a rolling pin to grind the sesame into powder. Add powdered sugar, flour and lard. Stir well and compress it on the kneading board. You can buy it in the supermarket nowadays.

第三步：在汤圆面中加入适量清水并揉匀，分成数坨，分别包入汤圆馅，做成圆球状的汤圆坯。

Step 3: Put some water into the tangyuan flour, then mix and knead. Divide it into pieces, and put the sesame filling in each piece. Knead it into a round ball.

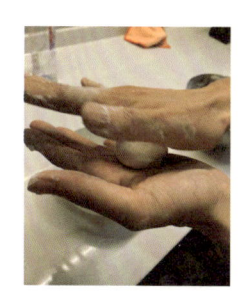

第四步：将大锅中的水烧开，放入汤圆。待汤圆浮起，加少许冷水，保持水面滚而不腾。汤圆翻滚，馅料熟化，皮软即熟。

Sept 4: Boil water with a big pot and put tangyuan into the water. While they are floating, add some cold water to prevent from overheating. Keep the tangyuan rolling without boiling. The tangyuan are cooked well while the inside is melting and the skin becomes soft.

第五步：食用时随上白糖、麻酱小碟，供蘸食用。

Sept 5: Then you can try it. If you eat with some sugar and sesame paste, the taste is better.

讲 中国故事　听 锦江声音 ——天府文化安逸行

Telling Stories of China and Listening to the Voice of Jinjiang —A Pleasant Journey of Tianfu Culture

项目展示与评价　Project Presentation and Evaluation

作品名称 Title of the work	
作品展示 Presentation	（照片粘贴 Stick the photo here）
作品评价 Evaluation	内容维度 Content：☆☆☆☆☆ 形式维度 Form：☆☆☆☆☆

项目感受　Reflection

说一说：汤圆在中国意味着团圆，对于这道甜蜜的成都美食，你有什么感受呢？

Share with us: tangyuan means reunion in Chinese traditional culture. After trying this, how do you feel about this sweet food in Chengdu?

第四单元　成都美食
Unit 4 Chengdu Tasty Foods

第五课　筋道喷香"男子汉"
——成都名小吃"甜水面"

Chewy and Fragrant Food
—Chengdu Famous Snack "Tianshui Mian"

你吃过有筷子那么粗、甜味中还有辣味的面条吗？

Have you ever had noodles that are as thick as chopsticks and taste sweet and spicy?

又甜又辣的粗面条？

Sweet and spicy thick noodles?

对！这就是成都的名小吃——甜水面！

Right! This is the famous snack of Chengdu—Tianshui Mian!

哇！真的很有特色！听起来就很好吃，不知道哪里能吃到呢？

Wow! It's really distinctive! It sounds delicious. I wonder where I can get it.

Telling Stories of China and Listening to the Voice of Jinjiang —A Pleasant Journey of Tianfu Culture

> 在靠近成都春熙路附近的西月城谭豆花，就能尝到正宗的甜水面。店内顾客络绎不绝，开放式的厨房也很卫生。
>
> Close to Chengdu Chunxi Road, there is a restaurant named "Xiyue City Tan Douhua". You can taste this authentic snack there! There is a steady stream of customers, and the open kitchen is clean.

项目介绍 Project Introduction

✧ 甜水面的历史
The history of Tianshui Mian

甜水面出现在清末，是成都市风味小吃中的"男子汉"。因为重用复制酱油、口味回甜而得名。粗壮的面条，具有硬朗、坚韧的风格，一上嘴就能感觉它的力度。加上红油辣椒、调味酱油、芝麻酱、蒜泥调味，吃起来感觉爽快，吃完后感觉痛快。

Tianshui Mian appeared in the late Qing Dynasty and was the "man" in local snacks of Chengdu. It got its name for using a special kind of soy sauce and its sweet aftertaste. The noodles are thick with a tough and tenacious style, and you can feel its strength once you try it. Also, with chili oil, seasoning sauce, sesame paste, and mashed garlic, you will feel refreshing while eating and feel happy and satisfied afterwards.

第四单元　成都美食

Unit 4 Chengdu Tasty Foods

项目任务 Task

你想尝试做一碗甜水面吗？

Do you want to try making a bowl of Tianshui Mian?

◇ 调制一碗甜水面
Make a bowl of Tianshui Mian

首先，我们来认识一下需要用到的材料。

First, let's see what ingredients are needed.

用料：	Ingredients:
面粉100克	100g flour
水50克	50g water
盐2克	2g salt
复制酱油4汤匙	4 spoons of cooked soy sauce
蒜泥5克	5g mashed garlic
香油1茶匙	1 spoon of sesame oil
辣椒红油2汤匙	2 spoons of chili oil
芝麻酱2汤匙	2 spoons of sesame paste
味精1/4茶匙	1/4 spoons of gourmet powder
香葱粒5克	5g green onions

第一步：在面粉中放入盐，分次加水并拌匀。揉成均匀的面团再饧15分钟。

Step1: Add salt into the flour, add water gradually, and mix them together. Knead it into a dough, and put aside for 15 minutes.

163

第二步：将烫好的面团放到案板上，擀成厚度约为5毫米的面片。

Step 2: Put the dough on a cutting board and roll it out to a thickness of about 5 mm.

第三步：切成宽度约为6毫米的面条。

Step 3: Cut into noodles for about 6 mm wide.

第四步：把面条抖散，两手抓住面条两头稍稍向两边扯长，放置在案板上。

Step 4: Shake the noodles, hold both ends of the noodles with two hands, and stretch them slightly to both sides. Put them on a cutting board.

第五步：小碗中先放入复制酱油，再放入辣椒红油和味精，调匀成味汁。把味汁分别放入两个碗中。

Step 5: Put the cooked soy sauce in the small bowl first, then add chili oil and gourmet powder, and mix well to make the sauce. Divide the sauce into two bowls.

第六步：锅中烧水，放入面条煮至八成熟，捞出后用香油拌匀后放凉。吃的时候将面条放入沸水中烫热，捞入碗中，淋入芝麻酱，撒上大蒜末和香葱粒拌匀即可。

Step 6: Boil water in a pot. Add noodles and cook them until 80% mature.

第四单元　成都美食
Unit 4 Chengdu Tasty Foods

Remove the noodles and mix them well with sesame oil, and let it cool. Heat the noodles in boiling water before eating, and put them in the bowl. Drizzle in sesame paste, sprinkle with mashed garlic and green onions, and mix them well.

项目展示与评价 Project Presentation and Evaluation

作品名称 Title of the work	
作品展示 Presentation	（照片粘贴 Stick the photo here）
作品评价 Evaluation	内容维度 Content：☆☆☆☆☆ 形式维度 Form：☆☆☆☆☆

165

讲中国故事 听锦江声音 ——天府文化安逸行
Telling Stories of China and Listening to the Voice of Jinjiang —A Pleasant Journey of Tianfu Culture

项目感受 Reflection

说一说：在亲自制作或者品尝了甜水面后，对于这道特别的成都美食，你有什么感受呢？

Share with us: after making or tasting Tianshui Mian, how do you feel about this special Chengdu food?

第四单元　成都美食
Unit 4 Chengdu Tasty Foods

第六课　下饭圣品——"回锅肉"

The Best Thing to Eat with Rice —"Twice-cooked Pork"

回锅肉是成都人民的下饭圣品。无论身处天南海北，无论吃着什么样的山珍海味，但是属于家乡的这道菜从未被忘记。

The twice-cooked pork is the best food for Chengdu people. No matter where you are, and no matter what kind of delicacies you have, this dish of hometown can never be forgotten.

哇！我口水直流了。

Wow! My mouth is watering.

那我们一起去探寻这道下饭圣品吧！

Then let's explore this together!

167

讲 中国故事　听 锦江声音　——天府文化安逸行
Telling Stories of China and Listening to the Voice of Jinjiang —A Pleasant Journey of Tianfu Culture

项目介绍 Project Introduction

◇ **回锅肉的历史**
The history of twice-cooked pork

回锅肉又叫"熬锅肉"，还被称作"爆肉"。关于回锅肉的历史尚未得到统一确认，但回锅肉的出现最早可以追溯到宋朝，在相关文学作品中已有提及。

Twice-cooked pork is also called "deep-fried pork", and also known as "explosive pork". The history of twice-cooked pork has not yet been unanimously confirmed, but the existence of twice-cooked pork can be traced back to Song Dynasty, when it has been mentioned in relevant literary works.

项目任务 Task

你想尝试做一盘回锅肉吗？

Do you want to try making a dish of twice-cooked pork?

◇ **炒一盘回锅肉**
Make a dish of twice-cooked pork

首先，我们来认识一下需要用到的材料。

First, let's see what ingredients are needed.

材料：	**Ingredients:**
● 二刀肉	● a piece of pork (in Sichuan, it's named "second knife")
● 青尖椒	● green pepper
● 洋葱	● onions
● 小米椒	● Capsicum frutescens
● 蒜苗	● garlic bolt
● 姜蒜末	● chopped ginger and garlic
● 豆瓣酱	● thick broad-bean sauce

第四单元　成都美食
Unit 4 Chengdu Tasty Foods

第一步：锅中加花椒、姜片、大葱段，并加入足量水烧沸。放入肉煮至七成熟捞出。

Step 1: Put Sichuan Pepper, ginger slices, green Chinese onions, and plenty of water into the pot. Add pork, cook until medium well, and then get it out.

第二步：晾凉后切成薄片。

Step 2: Let the pork cool and slice it thinly.

第三步：蒜苗洗净，斜切成段。红椒去蒂切菱形片。

Step 3: Wash the garlic bolt, and cut into segments. Cut red peppers into diamond slices.

169

讲 中国故事 听 锦江声音 ——天府文化安逸行
Telling Stories of China and Listening to the Voice of Jinjiang —A Pleasant Journey of Tianfu Culture

第四步：锅烧热后，放入肉片炒至出油。

Step 4: After heating up a pan, put pork slices and stir-fry until the lard is out.

第五步：另起锅，炒香姜蒜末。

Step 5: Heat up the other pan, and stir-fry the chopped ginger and garlic.

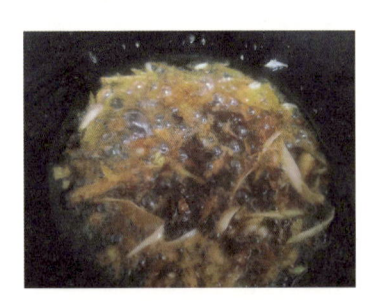

第六步：下入郫县豆瓣酱并炒香出红油。

Step 6: Add thick broad-bean sauce, and stir-fry until the chilli oil comes out.

第七步：倒入肉片，加入酱油翻炒均匀。

Step 7: Add pork slices and some soy sauce, and then stir them evenly.

第八步：加入洋葱、青尖椒等，再加入少许白糖调味。

Step 8: Add onions, green peppers, etc., and some sugar to add flavor.

第四单元　成都美食

Unit 4 Chengdu Tasty Foods

第九步：下入蒜苗、红椒翻炒后装盘即可。

Step 9: Add garlic bolt and red peppers. Stir-fry and dish up.

项目展示与评价 Project Presentation and Evaluation

作品名称 Title of the work	
作品展示 Presentation	（照片粘贴 Stick the photo here）
作品评价 Evaluation	内容维度 Content：☆☆☆☆☆ 形式维度 Form：☆☆☆☆☆

171

项目感受 Reflection

说一说：在制作回锅肉的过程中，你觉得哪些步骤比较难？

Share with us: what are the difficulties of making twice-cooked pork?